Simply Chomsky

Simply Chomsky

RAPHAEL SALKIE

SIMPLY CHARLY
NEW YORK

ISBN: 978-1-943657-70-4

Brought to you by http://simplycharly.com

Contents

Praise for *Simply Chomsky*

"Noam Chomsky's work has challenged and changed our understanding of the world, from his pioneering work in linguistics to his unceasing critique of the world around us. Raphael Salkie's book, *Simply Chomsky*, succeeds in bringing these critical issues to the attention of readers in a work at once succinct and illuminating."
   –Irene Gendzier, Professor Emeritus, Dept. of Political Science, Boston University

"Noam Chomsky is remarkably interesting and provocative–and therefore so is this book!"
   –Bill McKibben, author *Falter: Has the Human Game Begun to Play Itself Out?*

"Raphael Salkie has produced the most approachable, easy-to-read introduction to Noam Chomsky written so far. Speaking with a personal, very human voice, and peppered with Salkie's own up-to-date and illuminating examples, *Simply Chomsky* covers the major points of Chomsky's vast political output as well as his ground-breaking linguistics."
   –Milan Rai, author of *Chomsky's Politics*

"*Simply Chomsky* is a delightful book. Professor Salkie cuts through the many misconceptions that have surrounded Noam Chomsky, his political activism, and his views on language. Chomsky's thinking on education, the climate crisis, nuclear war, language evolution, and global political conflict, among other issues, is examined with refreshing clarity and perception. *Simply Chomsky* is a veritable cornucopia of the ideas of one of our most rational intellectuals and steadfast proponents of political change. It should be the starting point for readers who want to learn about Chomsky."

–Louise Cummings, Professor of Linguistics, Department of English, The Hong Kong Polytechnic University, Hong Kong SAR, China

"*Simply Chomsky* presents Chomsky's ideas in one concisely edited and accessible volume–a perfect introduction, chock full of nuggets and insights."

–David Barsamian, Alternative Radio

"An engaging and admirably succinct overview of Chomsky's vast output in linguistics and politics, *Simply Chomsky* offers a comprehensive, abundantly clear, and quite often funny survey of Chomsky's work. It deserves to be widely read not only by students and general readers, but also by those already familiar with Chomsky, who will appreciate the treatment of some less common themes. A call to political action as well as a discussion, this excellent synthesis will satisfy anyone looking for an accurate and accessible introduction to a figure of the first importance in both politics and intellectual life."

–Nick Riemer, Senior Lecturer in English and Linguistics Departments, University of Sydney

"Raphael Salkie has assembled a brief and accessible overview that will hopefully attract new readers to Noam Chomsky's work, where they will encounter a tremendous arsenal of ideas that can be employed to take on the plethora of issues we all face."

–Robert F. Barsky, author of *Noam Chomsky: A Life of Dissent* and Professor of French, English, and Law, Vanderbilt University

"This is a wonderfully lucid, accessible, and engaging introduction to Noam Chomsky's thought, which is a considerable feat. For decades, Chomsky has been both an insightful and inspirational analyst of modern politics and the most important figure in linguistics. The radical ideas that he introduced have completely recast our understanding of humans' capacity for language, with considerable implications for our view of human nature. Obviously, this is of great general interest, but much of Chomsky's work in linguistics is forbiddingly technical for the non-expert, and he has written so much on politics that it is hard to know where to start. By looking in detail at a few of the political areas where Chomsky has been active, Raphael Salkie builds up an impressively comprehensive picture of Chomsky's views and the libertarian and egalitarian ideals that underlie them. He goes to the heart of Chomsky's contribution to linguistics by giving the reader a guided tour of the most fundamental ideas and how they figure in contemporary theory. Throughout, Salkie's explanations are clear and illustrated with vivid examples."

–Nicholas Allott, Senior Lecturer of English Language, University of Oslo

Other *Great Lives*

Series Editor's Foreword

S imply Charly's "Great Lives" series offers brief but authoritative introductions to the world's most influential people–scientists, artists, writers, economists, and other historical figures whose contributions have had a meaningful and enduring impact on our society.

Each book provides an illuminating look at the works, ideas, personal lives, and the legacies these individuals left behind, also shedding light on the thought processes, specific events, and experiences that led these remarkable people to their groundbreaking discoveries or other achievements. Additionally, every volume explores various challenges they had to face and overcome to make history in their respective fields, as well as the little-known character traits, quirks, strengths, and frailties, myths, and controversies that sometimes surrounded these personalities.

Our authors are prominent scholars and other top experts who have dedicated their careers to exploring each facet of their subjects' work and personal lives.

Unlike many other works that are merely descriptions of the major milestones in a person's life, the "Great Lives" series goes above and beyond the standard format and content. It brings substance, depth, and clarity to the sometimes-complex lives and works of history's most powerful and influential people.

We hope that by exploring this series, readers will not only gain new knowledge and understanding of what drove these geniuses, but also find inspiration for their own lives. Isn't this what a great book is supposed to do?

Charles Carlini, Simply Charly
New York City

Acknowledgements

My family were hugely supportive and indulgent while I wrote this book, and sent me many suggestions for improvement. I am immensely grateful to them all.

Thanks to Sue Reed, Nick Riemer, and Nick Allott, who commented very helpfully on earlier drafts. Please don't assume that they agree with everything that I've written.

The person who introduced me to Chomsky's work, back when I was a first-year student, was François LeCercle. Then he was a "lecteur" in England for a year, and now he is a distinguished professor of literature in Paris. I send him a belated *merci mille fois*.

To Ilse Depraetere and Nicolas Ballier, I hope that this book repays some of the kindness that you have shown me over many years.

My former colleagues at the University of Brighton put up with my quirks and obsessions for a long time. I can only express the wish that their future is much less bleak than we all fear. A special mention for Mark Abel, Nadia Edmond, Trish McManus, Chris Cocking, Fiona MacNeill, and Tucker MacNeill: I couldn't have wished for better trade union activists at the University.

I am grateful to several anonymous Simply Charly readers for thoughtful comments, and to Helena Bachmann, my excellent copy editor.

Finally, thanks to Charles Carlini, a wise and patient publisher.

All errors and omissions are my responsibility alone.

Author-date System

When I refer to books and articles, I use the author–date system. In the "Sources" chapter at the end of this book, all these publications are listed in alphabetical order by author, and then in date order for each author. So to find out what "(Chomsky 2002)" refers to, find the Sources chapter and look under "C"; find Chomsky's name and then look down the years in chronological order until you reach 2002. This may seem a bit odd if you are not used to it, but it's a very efficient way to refer to written documents and web pages, and it is widely used in many fields.

Preface

Why another book about Chomsky?

L oved by many, hated by some: Noam Chomsky is an outspoken, world-renowned activist for social change. He is also a very distinguished scholar and linguist, whose work is admired by some, but denounced, ignored, and misunderstood by many others.

In addition, Chomsky is amazingly prolific. He has written over 120 books, along with vast numbers of articles, interviews, and videos. He corresponds with many people around the world: complete strangers often contact him, and he astonishes them with careful, detailed replies. Only the other day I switched on the BBC World Service on my radio and heard Chomsky, currently aged 91, speaking in his quiet but determined way about the Coronavirus crisis and other topics in the news.

A great deal has also been written about Chomsky. Some of it, in my opinion, is excellent and comprehensive (e.g. Smith and Allott 2016), some of it is poor (such as Collier and Horowitz 2004), and some of it is very good but a little out of date (for example, Rai 1995).

Simply Chomsky is short and therefore selective. It concentrates on Chomsky's preoccupations in the second decade of the 21st century, some of which look different from his earlier work. In a 2010 article, Chomsky wrote that his current research program about language "bars almost everything that has been proposed in the course of work on generative grammar" (2010a: 52). He is still asking the same questions, but he now thinks his previous answers to these questions can be abandoned, improved, or clarified—and he often moves into new areas, raising new research questions.

Another reason for a new book about Chomsky is that his work—about language and about social change—often challenges assumptions that are so widespread that they go unnoticed. What he says sometimes flies in the face of common sense, though for Chomsky that is not a problem if the statement is true, or at least supported by evidence. He comments that his ideas are so outlandish, they often sound like they come from the moon. It takes remarkable single-mindedness and strength of character to say things far outside the mainstream, and to do that for seven decades is extraordinary.

Many people find that reading Chomsky, or hearing him speak, feels like having your brain cleaned out and energized. This is surely a healthy thing, and I hope that this book can play a small part in supporting it.

About this book

Chomsky hates having books written about him. He gets no pleasure when people turn his surname into the adjectives *Chomskyan*, *Chomskyist* or *Chomskyite*, and he probably wishes that computer scientists didn't use *The Chomsky Hierarchy* as a technical term. He has always been an unpretentious academic, spending as much time as possible working quietly on linguistics in his office at MIT or, more recently, in Tucson, Arizona. I have written this book because I believe that Chomsky's political activities are important and because his linguistics is difficult for non-experts to understand when they start to study it. Another reason is that Chomsky has been the target of many myths, lies, and distortions throughout his adult life. The second chapter tries to set the record straight.

This book outlines Chomsky's life in Chapter 1, and returns to some of it in Chapter 3: his views on education were shaped largely by his personal experience as a young person and as a teacher. A good book that describes his life in more detail is *Noam Chomsky (Critical Lives)* by Wolfgang B. Sperlich (2006). I start with Chomsky's politics, which is of wider interest, and this part of the book takes up more space than the linguistics part. The hope is, nonetheless, that the chapters about language are a good beginning for anyone interested in Chomsky's latest work.

In the politics chapters, the focus is on Chomsky's concerns at the time of writing, that is, 2020. So the book says little about the political activity that first made Chomsky famous: his criticisms of the assault by the United States on Indochina (Vietnam, Laos, and Cambodia) from the 1950s to the 1970s. This remains by far the most destructive conflict since 1945, but it is over, though it continues to resonate and to mislead. Similarly, Central and South America have largely emerged from the US-backed military dictatorships of the past, and East Timor is no longer brutally occupied by Indonesia.

Shockingly, the consequences of the US-led attack on Korea in the 1950s continue to be in the news as I write, and the Israel-Palestine conflict shows little sign of a genuine resolution, so I deal with both of these, as Chomsky often has. The climate crisis, the threat of nuclear devastation, and the corruption of democracy in the United States are prominent in Chomsky's recent work, so they each get a chapter.

I wrote a longer book about Chomsky 30 years ago (Salkie 1990). It's quite good (of course, I would think that), but dated.

If you are ready to have your opinions and beliefs challenged—and sometimes condemned and ridiculed—then read on.

Raphael Salkie
Brighton, England

1. Chomsky's Life

"**N**oam Chomsky" is a difficult name. People often wonder if he is Russian (he isn't). They are not completely wrong, though: the surname is Slavic and the first name is Jewish.

His full name is Avram Noam Chomsky. He was born on December 7, 1928, in Philadelphia and raised in the city's East Oak Lane neighborhood. His parents, Elsie and William (Aliza and Ze'ev in Hebrew), were Jewish immigrants from the Russian empire. Chomsky speaks perfect English, though his father may have had a non-native accent because his first language was probably Yiddish.

Avram is the original Hebrew name of Abraham in the Jewish Bible, Abram in English (see *Genesis* 17:5 for the name change). *Noam* means "pleasantness" in Hebrew, and it is the male version of *Naomi*, who also first appeared in the Bible in the Book of *Ruth*. In Hebrew, the word has two syllables (*know-am*), but for English speakers, it is either pronounced with one syllable, so it sounds exactly like *gnome*, or with two, so that it rhymes with *know'em*. In the surname *Chomsky*, the *ch* is pronounced as in *church*. The name possibly comes from the town of Khomsk in Belarus (known as Chomsk in Polish), but that is not certain.

Early life

So much for the name. What about the person? Chomsky was born into a very actively Jewish family. It's important to clarify what "Jewish" means here because there is much more to it than just religion. Let's start with Noam's mother, Elsie Simonofsky (I am indebted to Feinberg [1999] for much of what follows). She was born in 1903 in Bobruisk, a town in Belarus. Its population at the time was about 40,000 people, 20,000 of whom were Jews. The town had organizations which reflected most of the currents of Jewish life in the Russian Empire: groups of Hasidim (members of a spiritual revivalist movement among very religious Jews); Misnagdim (followers of a highly intellectual form of Judaism—very religious but strongly opposed to the Hasidim); Zionists (advocates of a Jewish homeland in what was then Palestine); and Bundists (Jewish socialists who wanted a revolution and were intensely hostile to the Zionists). The town had a Yiddish theater, as well as many Jewish journals and newspapers.

Elsie was three years old when her mother took her and some of her siblings to the US, following her father, an uncle, and her oldest sister who had emigrated shortly before. Her father and mother were very religious, but Elsie and her siblings rebelled against their strict, traditional upbringing.

Noam's father, William "Welvel" Chomsky, was born in 1896 in Kupil (Yiddish Kopel), a village in the Ukraine, located roughly halfway between Kyiv (Kiev) in the East and Lviv (Lvov) in the West. Over half of the village's population at the time were Jews. When he was 17, the threat of forced conscription into the Tsar's army prompted William to move to the United States with his parents and two sisters, and they settled in Baltimore. William, like Elsie, rebelled against his Orthodox religious upbringing. But as Feinberg puts it, both he and Elsie were "committed to a Hebrew-nationalist culture based on the Hebrew language" (1999: 12).

Noam's parents were among over two million Jews who emigrated from the Russian Empire between 1880 and 1930, mostly to the United States. Some three million stayed behind, many of them later slaughtered by the Nazis. They were mainly descendants of Jews who had fled east from France and Germany in the Middle Ages to escape persecution. The majority were not allowed to live in Russia itself, and were restricted to Belarus, the Ukraine, and Poland, the area known in English as the "Pale of Settlement" (chertá osédlosti in Russian). They were distinct from their Christian neighbors in their religion, food, dress, and language: they spoke Yiddish, a variety of Medieval German, with some Slavic, and a few Hebrew and French words mixed in. But they prayed in Hebrew, the language of the

Bible. Yiddish was their "Mame Loshen" (mother language), while Hebrew was their "Loshen Kodesh" (holy language).

Over the centuries, life became steadily harder for these Jews. They mostly lived in grinding poverty, subjected to regular antisemitic attacks. Each area was required to supply a number of young men every year for the Russian army where they had to serve for 25 years. Religion gradually became less central for many Jews, though religious organizations remained fundamental for others. During the 19th century, modern influences–notably secular education, socialism, and the emancipation of women–competed with traditional religious beliefs.

For Noam's parents, the revival of Hebrew was the central Jewish element in their lives. Alongside Zionism, a movement emerged to rebuild Hebrew into a modern, spoken language with new words added that were not in the old religious texts. This was in part because of a feeling among American Jews that Yiddish was the language of poverty and discrimination back in the Pale–and for some, Yiddish was not a real language but just a "jargon," a pale imitation of German which had no place in the modern world. Elsie and William both devoted their lives to teaching Hebrew and training teachers of Hebrew, and William published several books, including *Hebrew, the eternal language* (W. Chomsky 1957), still regarded as one of the finest books on the subject. As a teenager, Noam helped his father prepare his books for publication, and Zionism was a regular topic of family conversation.

Noam's parents were thoughtful and progressive in their politics and believed that education should encourage young people to think for themselves and make the world a better place. So Hebrew and progressive ideas surrounded the young Chomsky, and as a teenager, he worked in Hebrew language summer camps for younger children. He wrote occasional articles in Hebrew in publications that his parents also wrote for, and one of his first pieces of writing in English was an essay about the Civil War in Spain for his school magazine.

Academic Career

After attending primary and high school in Philadelphia, Chomsky enrolled at the University of Pennsylvania (see Chapter 3 for more about his education). As a student there from 1945 to 1951, and then a Junior Fellow at Harvard for four years, Chomsky gradually came to believe that most of the work in linguistics at the time was totally misconceived.

In 1955, he took a job at the Massachusetts Institute of Technology (MIT) in Boston, where he worked on machine translation and developed his ideas about language. His first book, *Syntactic Structures* (Chomsky 1957) did not explicitly criticize other work in linguistics, but caused something of a stir; some people in the field suspected that something new and important was happening.

The first notable occasion when Chomsky went on the attack against current ideas in linguistics was at a conference in 1962, the Ninth International Congress of Linguists, held in Cambridge, Massachusetts. In his plenary lecture, later published as a book, Chomsky said:

> The central fact to which any significant linguistic theory must address itself is this: a mature speaker can produce a new sentence of his language on the appropriate occasion, and other speakers can understand it immediately, though it is equally new to them.

> [...]

> it is clear that a theory of language that neglects this "creative" aspect is of only marginal interest. (Chomsky 1964: 8)

Few people enjoy being told that their work is "of only marginal interest," and the controversy that followed was, to put it mildly, rather vigorous. Others rejected Chomsky's work in the field as "completely bankrupt" (Hockett 1968:3) and "an intellectual fraud"

(Gray 1977: 70), to pick out just two of the early insults. More recently, Larry Trask, a distinguished linguist working in the UK, dismissed the idea of Universal Grammar, a central notion in Chomsky's work, with these words:

> This stuff is so much half-baked twaddle, more akin to a religious movement than to a scholarly enterprise. I am confident that our successors will look back on Universal Grammar as a huge waste of time. (Brown 2003)

Before the 1962 Congress, Chomsky had written a devastating and often witty critique of a book by the psychologist B. F. Skinner (Chomsky 1959). He started by noting "the magnitude of [Skinner's] failure," and called Skinner's work "hopelessly premature," "futile," "misleading and unjustifiable," "confused," and "superficial."[1] This was psychology, though, not linguistics. Chomsky went on to criticize some leading contemporary philosophers, notably Hilary Putnam (see Chomsky 2000a, Chapter 2), as well as Willard Quine and Donald Davidson (Chomsky 2000a, Chapter 3).

Since those early days, Chomsky's linguistics has been admired by some, bitterly attacked by others, and misunderstood by many. In this book, I try to explain why—see Chapters 11 to 15.

In 1949, Chomsky married his childhood friend Carol Schatz. The couple visited a Kibbutz, a collective farming village, in Israel for several months, thinking about staying there, but Chomsky found the racism towards Arabs and the Stalinist politics repugnant, and they abandoned the idea. Chomsky has always kept his personal life away from the spotlight, but as far as I can tell, he and Carol had a happy life together until her death in 2008. They had three children: Aviva, born in 1957, is a professor of history and a political activist in Massachusetts. Diane, born in 1960, moved to Nicaragua in the 1980s to support the Sandinistas; she still lives there. She has worked for a charitable organization, Oxfam, in the region for many years. Harry, born in 1967, works as a musician and computer programmer in San Francisco.

In 2014, Chomsky married Valeria Wasserman, a translator from

Brazil 35 years his junior. Currently, they divide their time between Brazil and the United States. In 2018, Chomsky visited the former President of Brazil, Luiz Inácio Lula da Silva, who is in prison for what many see as unfair charges of corruption. In a letter to Lula after the visit, Chomsky described his imprisonment as "shameful," and added:

> The world badly needs a revival of the voice for the Global South that you were instrumental in facilitating as Brazil at last began to assume an effective role in the world stage under your leadership. (Chomsky 2018)

Chomsky stayed at MIT until 2017 when he took on a part-time post at the University of Arizona in Tucson. Over the course of his long career, he has received a huge number of prizes and awards. In a poll in 2005, conducted by the British magazine *Prospect* and the US magazine *Foreign Policy*, people were asked to name the world's leading public intellectual, and Chomsky was in first place.

Political activism

Chomsky's academic achievements are probably not the main reason for this popularity. On the other hand, his political writings, talks, and videos have a massive following. His view of the world took shape in his early years. As a child, he witnessed dreadful poverty in Philadelphia and saw the police attacking peaceful workers who were on strike. Although only a child at that time, he was aware of the growth of Fascism in Europe in the 1930s, and the horrors of the Civil War in Spain during the same decade. He experienced antisemitism in the streets from the local Irish Catholic and German communities—the latter included many active supporters of Adolf Hitler and the Nazis. He was almost 11 when the war broke out in Europe, and 13 when the US joined the war in 1941. The abuse local people directed at German prisoners of war in a camp near his home distressed him. The atom bombs dropped on Hiroshima and Nagasaki in 1945 appalled him.

As a teenager, Chomsky regularly visited New York City, where his uncle Milton had a newsstand on a street corner. Lots of people gathered nearby, and Chomsky joined in lively and interesting discussions about psychoanalysis, left-wing politics, and life in general. He had similar conversations in the bookshops nearby and at the New York office of the Yiddish language anarchist newspaper *Fraye Arbeter Shtime* (Free Voice of Labor).

In the early 1960s, Chomsky decided that he should devote much of his time and energy to political activism. Yet he was reluctant to do so, as he and his wife Carol had young children and a pleasant social life, and his academic work was having a big impact around the world. He knew that activism would take over much of his life. What's more, he was confident that the US government would hound him and he'd probably spend time in prison. To ensure that the family could survive financially, Carol went to graduate school at Harvard University and subsequently worked there.

It was a tough decision, but Chomsky felt that he could not look at himself in the mirror without shame if he just devoted himself to his academic career. Despite the risks, he was determined to stand with his students and friends who were opposed to the United States' assault on Vietnam, and who in many cases paid a heavy personal price for their refusal to serve in the US military. He did, indeed, spend a night in prison in 1967 (along with the writer Norman Mailer, and the prominent expert on childcare, Benjamin Spock) after a protest near the Pentagon. His name later appeared on President Richard Nixon's "Enemies List," and Chomsky only avoided criminal proceedings and a likely jail sentence because of the ineptitude of the FBI.

For decades, Chomsky has spoken in public all over the world. Often he will speak to an academic audience about language one day, and a more diverse audience about politics the next day. For a good example of this, look at Chomsky (1987) and (1988), based on talks he gave in Managua, the capital of Nicaragua: a book about politics, and a book about language and knowledge, one published by a small left-wing publisher, the other by a major University Press. He has a calm, not at all flamboyant style when he speaks in public and a dry sense of humor which is not always evident in his writing. He insists that his aim is to help people think for themselves, not to persuade them by the power of his rhetoric.

2. Myths

> Chomsky is a sarcastic, angry, soporific, scowling, sneering self-hating Jew, devoid of hope and speaking from hell, whose alpha-male brutality drives him to win at all costs, and who imposes on the world disappointingly crude and simplistic arguments to the point where he is so inconsequential that one wonders whether he has ever changed even a single thing in his 60 years of political work. (Glenn Greenwald in The Guardian, a liberal UK newspaper, 2013)

Strong, nasty words. Luckily, Glenn Greenwald, an outstanding anti-establishment journalist, doesn't believe any of them. He calls them "horrible slurs" and "caricatures," and the point of his article is to ridicule them.

Where does this abuse come from? Sadly, it was incited by an article written by Aida Edemariam in the same British newspaper, The Guardian, published a few days before. The article described Chomsky's talk to a packed audience in London as "a monotone, ... almost soporific" and "disappointingly crude and simplistic." Edemariam mentioned Chomsky's "sarcasm" three times and quoted a similar sneery attack on him in the liberal New Yorker magazine (MacFarquhar 2003), which she described as "a brilliant profile": "Chomsky's sarcasm is the scowl of a fallen world, the sneer of hell's veteran to its appalled naifs." (Don't worry about the words appalled naifs: they aren't worth it). Edemariam asked: "Does he think that in all these years of talking and arguing and writing, he has ever changed one specific thing?"

Greenwald dismisses all these insults, as we will see in a moment, but the important thing is this: you would expect fierce attacks on Chomsky in the right-wing press. He is, after all, a world-famous and prolific left-wing activist who can be described as radical, socialist, progressive, anarchist, critical, revolutionary, and subversive. Chomsky sometimes attacks the US Republican party, describing it as "the most dangerous organization in history" (see Chapter 10). But his primary target, in fact, is not the political right-wing but the so-called "liberal" or "moderate" center, which likes to think of itself as enlightened and progressive: Barack Obama, Bill Clinton, and–long ago now–John Kennedy, Lyndon Johnson, and Jimmy Carter. When he had to choose between Hillary Clinton and Donald Trump in 2016, he chose Clinton as the lesser of two evils (Halle & Chomsky 2016)–but the lesser evil is still evil and in some ways the more dangerous evil, for reasons that we will explore in Chapter 5.

Narrow Choices

What Chomsky objects to most strongly is a picture of the world which narrows the range of political choices to two: center-right and center-left. In the US, these have traditionally been the Republicans and the Democrats; in the UK, the Conservative and Labour Parties. The problem is that these two political perspectives share certain beliefs and assumptions which are rarely challenged in mainstream debate and reporting. Often they disagree, of course, sometimes passionately, but the noisy arguments conceal basic agreements that are not mentioned: they are just taken for granted. Here are some examples:

- From the 1950s to the early 1970s, the US waged a vicious war against Vietnam and neighboring countries. It was the most destructive armed conflict since 1945, with over three million deaths, more than seven million tons of bombs dropped by the US Air Force (compared with two million tons by all sides in the whole of World War II), and huge areas poisoned by US chemical weapons and littered with unexploded US bombs. The center-right "hawks" thought the US would win the war.

The center-left "doves" were pessimistic. The basic assumption shared by the hawks and the doves was that the invasion (a term that they never used, of course) was legitimate. The voices which said that the invasion was immoral and evil, were marginalized.

- In 2003, there was a fierce debate in the US and the UK about how to remove the evil Iraqi dictator Saddam Hussein and his notorious Weapons of Mass Destruction (WMDs). Should we bomb him, or should we negotiate? The shared assumption was that we had the right to intervene. The voices that said the war was immoral and a thinly veiled theft of Iraq's oil and gas resources, and that there were no WMDs in Iraq, were marginalized and ignored. The same voices warned (rightly, as everyone can now see) that the invasion would cause devastation and chaos across the region.

Chomsky gets abused by liberals because he challenges these shared assumptions. They will agree with him up to a point and say some nice things about him: Edemariam referred to "his extraordinary range of reference and experience." But when he mentions that liberals are also responsible for many of the world's evils, it isn't surprising that they don't like it and fight back—often viciously.

Greenwald dismisses this abuse:

> What's particularly strange about this set of personality and style attacks is what little relationship they bear to reality. Far from being some sort of brutal, domineering, and angry "alpha-male" savage, Chomsky—no matter your views of him—is one of the most soft-spoken and unfailingly civil and polite political advocates on the planet. [...] But the strangest attack on Chomsky is the insinuation that he has changed nothing. [...] I'd say that there is no living political writer who has more radically changed how more people think in more parts of the world about political issues than he. If you

accept the premise (as I do) that the key to political change is to convince people of pervasive injustice and the need to act, then it's virtually laughable to depict him as inconsequential.

In the rest of his article, Greenwald asks why Chomsky is often described in this way, and his answer is that Chomsky says things that powerful people do not like. Instead of responding to what trouble-makers say, powerful people often belittle them by attacking their personality and their way of speaking, and by misrepresenting or caricaturing their message.

Making a difference

I should add a comment that Chomsky often makes: very few individuals change the world alone (indeed, that's the title of Edemariam's article, where his reply to her facile remark is in the same vein). Chomsky's activism is part of the hard work, courage, and determination of innumerable people around the world. Many of them are not well known, and too many of them are imprisoned, tortured, exiled, or impoverished because of their commitment to freedom, peace, and justice.

That said, here are two among countless examples of "specific things" where Chomsky has personally made a difference:

- In 1971, Chomsky played an important part in publishing the Pentagon Papers. These secret official documents showed that the US government had repeatedly and deliberately lied about its assault on Vietnam. They were crucial in turning public opinion against the war.
- In 2002, Chomsky (then aged 73) flew to Turkey to support the publisher Fatih Tas, who was on trial for "producing propaganda against the unity of the Turkish state" and faced a prison sentence if found guilty. Tas had published an essay by Chomsky. He was acquitted, and said later that "if Chomsky

hadn't been here we wouldn't have expected such a verdict."
(BBC News, 2002)

Choice of words

Let's take a closer look at the language of Edemariam's article. "Sarcastic" is an interesting word to describe Chomsky. When he speaks in public, he frequently makes humorous remarks about powerful people or institutions (the late, much-loved UK politician Tony Benn regularly did the same). For example, Chomsky often describes opinions in newspapers read by businesspeople—the *Wall Street Journal* or the British *Financial Times*, for example—as "vulgar Marxism." (e.g. Chomsky 2014: 113) This term is normally used to criticize people on the left whose view of the class struggle is crude and simplistic: the noble "proletarians" versus the evil "bosses." Using it to describe simplistic class war talk by the "bosses" usually gets a laugh from Chomsky's audience. (Chomsky is deadly serious about this: he talks often about "a highly class-conscious business system which is always fighting an intense and self-conscious class war;" see Chomsky 1994: 48.) That's how humor often works: use an expression in an unusual context and then wait for the audience to realize that the expression works in a topsy-turvy but informative way. A sympathetic reporter could have described this as "witty," rather than "vicious sarcasm"—the term used in *The New Yorker*. The reporters in *The Guardian* and *The New Yorker* had a choice, and they chose the negative expression.[1]

What about "soporific," in other words, boring, to describe Chomsky's speaking manner? I have seen Chomsky speak several times (and there are many videos on the internet), and most of his audience manages to stay awake. More importantly, Chomsky repeatedly says that you should distrust anyone who makes impassioned speeches. People on both ends of the political spectrum used this tactic—for instance, fascists like Adolf Hitler and Benito Mussolini on the right, and Bolsheviks Vladimir Lenin and Leon Trotsky on the left. No doubt emotions, such as anger about injustice and compassion for its victims, should play a part in political action, but only if they are guided by careful thought and discussion. Chomsky wants people to think for themselves, not to be swayed by his rhetoric.

Liberal media

In between this and the other dismissive language–gathered together in the first Greenwald quote above–the earlier articles in *The Guardian* and *The New Yorker* included some positive accounts of Chomsky's views. The liberal and left-of-center media are like that: they mix fair coverage of people like Chomsky with sneery attacks on their personality and style–sometimes in the same article. If the Edemariam piece had not included sneers and slurs, it would no doubt have been accused of "hagiography." This insult, which originally meant "a story about a Christian saint," later came to mean "a biography which treats its subject with undue reverence," and now is used to denigrate a fair article about someone that the speaker doesn't like. *The Guardian* deserves praise for publishing Greenwald's response–but shame on them for publishing the partly dreadful piece by Edemariam a few days earlier.

Incidentally, *The Guardian* has "form" (lawyer-speak for "previous crimes") on Chomsky. In 2005, the paper published a piece about him (Brockes 2005), for which they later apologized after worldwide protests. Chomsky described this article as "a very impressive effort, which obviously took careful planning and work, to construct an exercise in defamation that is a model of the genre," and warned people that "if you accept [an] invitation [from *The Guardian* for an interview], be cautious, and make sure to have a tape recorder that is very visibly placed in front of you. That may inhibit the dedication to deceit, and if not, at least you will have a record" (Chomsky 2005).

Myths and Reality

What about the other insults on Greenwald's list? I'll ignore the ones that refer to Chomsky's personality and speaking manner: this book has nothing more to say about that. Some of them, though, are about Chomsky's political activities. They are among a cluster of widespread myths about Chomsky, and it is useful to clear them out of the way.

Myth 1: Chomsky's political views are "disappointingly crude and simplistic."

The reality

If you want genuinely crude and simplistic views, look no further than the founders of the world's great religions: Buddha, Confucius, Moses, Mohammed, Jesus, etc. "Thou shalt not steal" and "Love thy neighbor as thyself" are hardly subtle and sophisticated.

In his linguistics and political activities, Chomsky often makes remarks which he himself calls "truisms"–statements that are obviously true and say nothing new or controversial. Here are two examples:

- The foreign policy of a country is largely shaped by powerful elites within that country.
- The only coherent notion of "a language" (English, Punjabi, etc), taken for granted by everyone, is a biological one.

He notes that these banal assertions are often rejected in practice. What you find instead are these assumptions, either unstated or explicit:

- American foreign policy is an attempt, sometimes unsuccessful, to promote freedom, democracy, human rights, and prosperity throughout the world.
- Language is basically a means of communication.

Chomsky dismisses both of these assumptions as false and dangerous. Insisting on unpopular truisms is a way to make powerful enemies. It is also, many people find, a good way to stay rational when you are thinking about difficult problems.

Here is another example. Chomsky often speaks about "terrorism," pointing out that one of the best ways to reduce its incidence in the world is to not engage in it—as the US and its allies do on a massive scale. This is crude and simplistic, but just like the quotes from Moses and Jesus, it is in my view true and worth saying, because it cuts through a lot of the shallow discussion of terrorism in the mainstream media and in academic studies.

On top of this, Chomsky's political writings are, notoriously, supported by masses of detailed evidence and references to sources, including internal US government documents. The same is less true of his talks, of course—you can't do that as much when you speak in public.

Myth 2: Chomsky is "a self-hating Jew."

The reality

Chomsky is Jewish, and in his early years, Israel and Palestine were a hot topic for him, his friends, and his family. He has written a lot about the Middle East, and has been severely critical of successive Israeli governments, arguing that their policies towards Palestinians are brutal and, in the long run, possibly suicidal, a view that I share. He points out that his opinions are commonplace in Israel, and that they reflect an international consensus about how to end the occupation of the West Bank and the wider conflict—a consensus which unfortunately is opposed by elites in Israel and the United States.

It is not unusual for supporters of Israel to describe Jewish critics of Israeli policies as "self-hating Jews" (or antisemites—see below). The term is an interesting one. In Greenwald's article, he notes that Edemariam says that Chomsky was described as "America's most prominent self-hating Jew" by the left-wing *Nation* magazine. Greenwald traced the source of this statement and found that the article in *The Nation* used the term only to debunk this accusation in the same sentence. *The Guardian* later removed and apologized for this slur.

What does the term mean? The claim is surely not that Chomsky hates himself, but rather that he hates being Jewish—and, by extension, all Jewish culture, religion, communal institutions, and Israel. Well, I am also Jewish, and I can assure you that lots of Jews hate some other Jews, and particular aspects of Jewish culture, religion, communal institutions, and Israel, with undisguised vehemence. Jewish newspapers are full of internal conflict. There are even jokes about it, like the one about the Jew who goes to a desert island and builds two synagogues. The first is the synagogue he goes to, and the other is the one that he wouldn't set foot in. More seriously, in 1999 an incident of genuine Jewish self-hatred occurred in Jerusalem, as reported in *The New York Times*:

> In an ugly confrontation 100 strictly Orthodox [Jewish] yeshiva students surrounded a group of American Reform rabbis who went to pray at the Western Wall this morning, booing loudly and hurling insults past officers from the border police.

What was most chilling to the Americans was that the youths, their faces contorted in anger under their black hats, screamed that the rabbis should "go back to Germany," to be exterminated, one explained later. (Sontag, 1999)

Why do some Jews hate some other Jews? The answer is simple: antisemitism—the vicious oppression of Jews simply for being Jewish. The slaughter of millions of Jews by the Nazis was the most extreme episode in a long history of this disgusting hatred, which has included defamation, lower-class civil status, being forced to live in ghettos, forced expulsion, and murder for hundreds of years. It is deeply ingrained in every society, and all Jews carry the fear of it in their lives. This fear often finds expression in distrust of other Jews.

That is not unusual. Oppressed groups typically have a tendency to feel powerless and to blame themselves and other members of the group for their mistreatment. The great South African activist Steve Biko, murdered by the Apartheid Regime in 1977, understood this "internalized oppression" clearly: He famously said that "the most potent weapon in the hands of the oppressor is the mind of the oppressed," and he argued that black people needed to overcome their feelings of inferiority so they could see themselves as worthy and fully human, not just "appendages to the white society." The same problem of "self-hatred" is found in other victims of oppression, such as women, gay men and lesbians, working-class people, and others. It is certainly not unique to Jews. The use of the term "self-hating Jew" by one Jew about another should be seen as part of this phenomenon—and not taken as a serious criticism of Chomsky.

Let's look at some more widespread myths about Chomsky's politics.

Myth 3: Chomsky has endorsed Holocaust denial.

The reality

Chomsky has never denied the Holocaust. If you believe in free speech, he says, then you have to apply the principle to views you detest. You can challenge, criticize, or ridicule such views, but that is different from saying that people who express these views should be sent to prison. He, therefore, supports the civil rights of Holocaust deniers like Robert Faurisson and David Irving, which is different from endorsing what they say. As well as this principled position, tactical considerations for anyone on the left lead to the same conclusion: if you allow governments to imprison someone for their political opinions, anyone who criticizes the government is liable to end up in jail. At the time of this writing, Turkey is a good example of a country where expressing one's views can result in arbitrary imprisonment: the German broadcaster Deutsche Welle noted recently that "Turkey leads the world in imprisoned journalists and continues to arrest anyone who voices opposition to the Erdogan government" (Deutsche Welle 2020).

Myth 4: Chomsky refused to condemn the brutal atrocities of the Khmer Rouge regime in Cambodia.

The reality

The Khmer Rouge took power in 1975 and were ousted by the Vietnamese army in 1979. A book by Chomsky and Edward Herman, called *After the Cataclysm, Postwar Indochina and the Reconstruction of Imperial ideology*, appeared in 1979. Part of the book examined how the Khmer Rouge regime was reported in the United States and compared that with the reporting of similar atrocities carried out during the same period by the Indonesian regime in East Timor. In the case of Cambodia, news and statistics were fabricated and exaggerated. East Timor was barely mentioned. Another omission was the devastation of Cambodia before 1975 by US bombing, with estimates of deaths between 250,000 and over a million (for a good discussion, see World Peace Foundation, 2015).

In the case of Cambodia, when the book appeared, it was too late to do anything about the Khmer Rouge. The East Timor slaughter, in contrast, continued until 2000, with US support. At any point, the US could have intervened to stop these massacres, and that is, of course, also true of the US bombing before 1975.

So Chomsky was more concerned with atrocities that he could do something about (those carried out by the US or with US support) than with atrocities about which he could do nothing. He has often said that "condemning" crimes committed by official enemies is easy, and usually does little to help the victims—another "truism," though widely ignored in practice. Here is one example:

> Nothing is easier than to shed responsibility, to condemn the crimes—often real—of someone else. There is much that could have been done to present a fair and honest picture of what was and had been happening, and to change [...] U.S. Policies [...] To the extent that we do not do what can be done, we have only ourselves to blame for the consequences. If these are truisms, and they are, they nevertheless will bear repetition so long as they are ignored. (Chomsky 1999a: 667)

Myth 5: Chomsky is vehemently "anti-American."

The reality

Chomsky often says that the United States is an exceptionally free society, where people like him can say what they want and organize opposition to the government, usually without fear of punishment or repression. Few other countries come close. Wealthy people in the US—and he includes himself here—can enjoy a very pleasant lifestyle. He also points out, forcibly, that to label someone "anti-American" betrays a totalitarian mindset in which slavish obedience to the establishment is assumed to be normal. I doubt that terms such as "anti-Czech" (13,000 hits on Google, mostly referring to the Nazi period) or "anti-Djibouti" (one hit on Google) are currently widespread. We should dismiss the label as laughable and contemptible.

In many other countries, people who criticize the government face harassment, imprisonment, or worse. That such things are rare in the United States places a special responsibility on citizens of that country: they cannot use fear of these consequences as an excuse for not speaking out about injustice.

Chomsky writes a lot about the United States and is often very negative. He says that it is easy and safe to be critical of countries, political systems, and people far away. Sadly, anything you say or do about them is likely to make little difference. What you say or do about your own neighborhood, town or country can make a difference. In particular, you should apply the same guiding principles to your own community that you apply to others—in fact, you should be tougher on your own community. These are more "truisms," which are often rejected in practice. I agree with him.

Myth 6: Chomsky is an anarchist, and therefore

supports violent action to overthrow the US government.

The reality

Chomsky has never advocated political violence. In fact, he has repeatedly condemned it as morally wrong, tactically disastrous, and a lazy alternative to painstaking left-wing organizing. He has often said that violent protest is likely to be a tactical error, for two reasons: firstly, because it allows those in power to demonize the protesters, making it harder to get widespread popular support. Secondly, the rich and powerful are better at violence than "regular" people. It makes sense to use tactics that are more likely to lead to victories. (Compare the points about free speech above.)

Chomsky says that organizing, particularly in trade unions but also in churches and other community groups, is the key to positive political change. If he thinks his vote will make a difference, he votes in elections. He sees no contradiction between working for piecemeal reform, which can improve the lives of real people here and now, and large-scale social revolution.

He writes:

> [we should] extend the democratic system to investment, the organization of work, and so on. That would constitute a major social revolution, which, in my view at least, would consummate the political revolutions of an earlier era and realize some of the libertarian principles on which they were partly based. (Chomsky 1989: 7)

For more on Chomsky's anarchism, see chapter 3.

Now for some myths about Chomsky's linguistics, starting with the most important one.

Myth 7: Chomsky's insights into language have been central to his political activism.

The reality

There are no significant links between Chomsky's linguistics and his politics. You need not know anything at all about Chomsky's linguistics to understand his political views. He always separates the two, and when asked–as often happens–about connections, he just makes some mundane remarks about keeping an open mind and being critical. Linguistics is a complex and technical field: to master it, you need to study hard, think about abstract concepts, and engage in detailed hands-on research. Political activism is not complex and not technical: it needs compassion, courage, stamina, and a willingness to listen, but no special intellectual training or talent.

Some of Chomsky's finest supporters don't agree with me on this point: Carlos Otero, Jean Bricmont, Robert Barsky, Neil Smith, and Nicholas Allott have all tried to link Chomsky's linguistics and his politics (as I did too, after lengthy health warnings, in my 1990 book). I seem to be in a small minority when I say that the links are trivial–though another member of the minority is Chomsky himself, whose view on the matter should probably carry some weight.

Myth 8: Chomsky is very important because he has "revolutionized" the study of language.

The reality

Chomsky has always maintained that his work is a minority interest within the field of linguistics, and this is accurate. Linguistics–the scientific study of language–is a wide and diverse subject. It includes the social aspects of language, the history of languages, how we use language (pragmatics), how to learn and teach languages, using computers to process language, and other areas where Chomsky's influence has been limited. His approach to linguistics is important and worth learning about, but you should distrust claims about his revolutionary impact.

Conferences about pragmatics, or language and computers, often attract more than 1000 participants. Conferences on Chomsky's type of linguistics tend to be much smaller affairs.

People who claim that Chomsky's linguistics is influential sometimes say that he has been cited by other researchers more than any other living person. This crude statistic does not tell us how many of the people who refer to Chomsky actually understand him correctly. Of those who do, the majority are probably hostile or dismissive.

The next time you read a book that tells you that Chomsky "revolutionized" linguistics, I suggest that you remember the words of the 18th-century philosopher David Hume and "commit it to the flames"–or at least, take it back to the library.

Myth 9: Key terms in Chomsky's current work include *transformational grammar, deep structure versus surface structure, competence versus*

performance, "Language Acquisition Device" (LAD), "ideal speaker-listener," core grammar and periphery, "government" "binding," the "cycle," and X-bar Theory.

The reality

Chomsky has not used these terms for some years, and I don't use them in this book. There are many books that outline the history of Chomsky's work in linguistics, notably Smith & Allott (2016). *Simply Chomsky* concentrates on his current ideas at the time of writing.

Why so many myths?

There are several reasons. Among the less important ones are the poor quality of some scholarship in the humanities and social sciences, and awe (perhaps including envy) at Chomsky's exceptional ability to write, speak in public, and do research, even at the age of 91.

A more interesting reason is the widespread hostility, often amounting to vitriolic abuse, aimed at Chomsky in both areas. In relation to his political work, Chomsky and his collaborator Edward Herman have proposed a "Propaganda Model" which predicts this hostility—cf. Chapter 5. In linguistics, the hostility often arises because Chomsky's approach to language seems to many people to fly in the face of common sense. He accepts that this is true, but doesn't see it as a flaw in his work—cf. Chapter 11.

The hostility also has something to do with the nature of education in the United States and similar advanced industrial countries. Chomsky has written extensively about education, and it's a good place to start looking at his ideas in more detail—as we do in the next chapter.

A final word

As an antidote to Edemariam's abuse and Greenwald's irony, here's another quote from someone who knows Chomsky well.

> I first met Noam Chomsky in 1966, when I was a student at MIT. [...] Even more impressive than his prodigious intelligence has been his extraordinary commitment to social change. As an undergraduate, I was struck that such a distinguished scholar would join with students at sit-ins and demonstrations. In the early 1970s when I was working on a small newsletter challenging martial law in the Philippines, the first subscription renewal we'd receive in the mail each year was from Noam Chomsky. This has been a consistent pattern as long as I've known him. He has helped innumerable political organisations and publications, answered countless letters from around the globe, and taken the time to talk to, advise, and inspire all those struggling for a better world. *Stephen Shalom*, Preface to Chomsky & Achcar (2007, p viii)

3. Education

[At my first school] children were encouraged to challenge everything, and you sort of worked on your own, you were supposed to think things through for yourself–it was a real experience. The ethos at my High School was different: highly competitive and fostering conformity: it was the dumbest, most ridiculous place I've ever been, it was like falling into a black hole or something. (NC in Mitchell & Schoeffel 2002: 237)

C homsky's views on education are strongly influenced by his own experiences. Between the ages of two and 12, he attended Oak Lane Country Day School in his hometown of Philadelphia. This unusual school was based on the ideas of John Dewey (1859–1952), a leading American philosopher and educational reformer. A useful outline of Dewey's thinking is Dewey (1986), an article that contains short extracts from his 1938 book *Experience and Education*. He contrasted traditional education with a progressive approach:

The main purpose or objective [of traditional education] is to prepare the young for future responsibilities and for success in life, by means of acquisition of the organized bodies of information and prepared forms of skill which comprehend the material of instruction. Since the subject-matter as well as standards of proper conduct are handed down from the past, the attitude of pupils must, upon the whole, be one of docility, receptivity, and obedience.

... we may, I think, discover certain common principles amid the variety of progressive schools now existing. To imposition from above is opposed expression and cultivation of individuality; to external discipline is opposed free activity; to learning from texts and teachers, learning through experience; to acquisition of isolated skills and techniques by drill, is opposed acquisition of them as means of attaining ends which make direct vital appeal; to preparation for a more or less remote future is opposed making the most of the opportunities of present life; to static aims and materials is opposed acquaintance with a changing world. (Dewey 1986: 243-4)

Dewey was also struck by the undemocratic nature of traditional education, where the teachers or lecturers make the rules and decide what is "learnt," and the students have very little, if any, power over what happens.

A modern interpreter of Dewey put it like this:

Dewey undertook to rethink education not as a limited transmission of the highest achievements of the past from a few to a few, but as discipline of and practice in creative adaptation through solving problems in living for the good of each and for all. Thus, education also became for him, a process of enhancing living, rather than preparation for life, as if living were something that could be deferred until we, some of us, have been trained and made ready for it. This, Dewey thought, was as absurd as it is pernicious. (Minnich 2006: 150)

Chomsky is a great admirer of Dewey's views on education (and also on democracy–see Chapter 9), though elsewhere he criticizes him and his circle sharply for "[taking] great pride, as you can see from their own writings at the time, in having shown that what they called the 'more intelligent members of the community,' namely, themselves, were able to drive a reluctant population into [the First World War] by terrifying them and eliciting jingoist fanaticism." (Chomsky 1997: 8)

Against rote learning

One of Chomsky's basic principles—that received ideas and institutions should be challenged, rather than accepted unthinkingly—derives in part from his experiences at his first school. His views were also strongly influenced, this time in a negative way, by his teenage years. From the age of 12, Chomsky attended Central High School in Philadelphia, but he did not appreciate it, as the quote above makes clear. Competitive rote learning struck him as unpleasant and pointless. As a teenager, he learned a lot more away from school: from conversations within his family, reading widely, helping with his father's books about Hebrew, personal experience, and last but not least, his regular visits to New York City (see Chapter 1).

Chomsky enrolled at the University of Pennsylvania in 1945. He attended classes that interested him, rather than worrying about course requirements. He studied philosophy, logic, and languages, but was losing interest in these subjects. He was considering dropping out of formal education and moving to a kibbutz in Israel when he met Professor Zellig Harris (1915–1992). Harris was a leading figure in linguistics who shared Chomsky's interest in left-wing Jewish politics. Harris's teaching methods were unorthodox: he preferred to meet students in bars and cafés rather than in lecture halls. Chomsky helped to prepare Harris's book, *Methods in Structural Linguistics*, for publication in 1951. He went on to get a Master's Degree in linguistics, and the rest is history.

Apprenticeship

What does this show us? Firstly, that Chomsky himself learned most successfully as an amateur, outside the formal system of exams and qualifications. He learned a lot from spending time with people whose ideas caught his interest and imagination. He has often said that the best way to learn a hard subject like linguistics is to engage in it as an apprentice, picking up from the experts the key techniques and the sense of which research questions are worth pursuing.

What's more, from his early schooling and the lively conversations in New York, Chomsky learned that ideas and theories are there to be scrutinized, tested, and challenged. That is how progress is made in any field of study. When education is just learning established facts and theories, the assumption is that the human mind needs to be filled with water like a vessel. That didn't work for Chomsky, and he thinks it is the wrong approach in general. He believes that real education is about helping people to think for themselves. Referring to Dewey, Chomsky summarizes these ideas as:

> The view that education is not to be viewed as something like filling a vessel with water, but rather assisting a flower to grow in its own way (in other words, providing the circumstances in which the normal creative patterns will flourish). (Otero 2003: 26)

Chomsky likes to refer to Wilhelm von Humboldt (1767-1835), the German linguist and educational reformer. Humboldt thought education should be seen as laying out a string along which young people will develop, each in her or his own way, with some guidance from experts where necessary. As a researcher, Chomsky has tried to put these ideas into practice:

> Anyone who teaches science, at least at an advanced level, is perfectly aware of the fact that you don't lecture. You may be standing in front of a room, but it's a cooperative enterprise. Studying is more a form of apprenticeship than anything else. It's kind of like learning to be a skilled carpenter. You work with somebody who knows how to do it. Sometimes you get it, sometimes you don't get it. If you get it, you're a skilled carpenter. How it's transmitted, nobody can say.

Science is a lot like that. You just sort of have to get it. The way you get it is by interacting. The same is true here. You go to a class in linguistics and it's a discussion. The people sitting in the seat where you're sitting are usually so-called students who are talking about things, teaching me about what they've discovered. (Chomsky & Barsamian 1996: 42)

The stupidity of "intellectuals"

Now for some ideas that are hard to accept but make sense if you think about them. Chomsky argues that the most highly "educated" people in the current system are usually the most indoctrinated, most ignorant, and most stupid because they are exposed to the most propaganda—in fact, they are often involved in creating this propaganda (see Chapter 5). These are the people who struggle with the "truisms" that we started to describe in Chapter 2. Highly "educated" people are often confident speakers, use long words, and talk about abstract things. They write thoughtful newspaper columns and profound books, and they take each other very seriously. They think of themselves as intelligent, far-sighted, and sophisticated (as opposed to ordinary people, who are none of these things). Chomsky argues that they have seen themselves as managers—either of industry, a state, or an ideology. They internalize the propaganda and believe it, often without realizing it.

As evidence that "ordinary people" can see things more clearly than elites, Chomsky often refers to opinion polls in the US which ask people whether the American assault on Vietnam in the 1960s and 70s was a "mistake" or "fundamentally wrong and immoral." (Spoiler alert: it was the latter). Among the general population, over 70 percent go for wrong and immoral, compared to about 40 percent among "opinion leaders." (see Chomsky 1987: 64 for one example) He also tells us not to be misled by the assertion that intellectuals were often the most prominent critics of the war.

Firstly, the intellectuals were the minority. Secondly, "as in the case of most popular movements, the effective grassroots activists are unknown to the general public, or to history" (Chomsky 1987: 67).

Opinion polls also show, Chomsky points out, that the overwhelming majority of US citizens want universal healthcare and would prefer the United States to work closely with international organizations like the United Nations to end conflicts and promote peace and development. They support women's right to access abortion, and want stricter gun control. In one of his favorite polls, many respondents thought the words "from each according to their ability, to each according to their needs" were from the US Constitution and not from their real source—the Communist philosopher and economist Karl Marx.

Rational and irrational

Two of the crucial words that Chomsky uses time and again are *rational* (based on reason, evidence, and logic) and *irrational* (well over 50 occurrences in the books cited in this chapter, in case you're interested).

Here's an example of what he means: the climate crisis. The vast majority of scientists argue that the build-up of greenhouse gases is real and dangerous. The giant oil companies, on the other hand, have spent huge amounts of money supporting organizations like the Heritage Foundation who take the opposite view (for some figures, see Greenpeace 2019). Now there are two possible ways to think about this. The climate deniers claim that the scientists are misleading us because they want fame, prestige, and money for their research (for an example, see Plimer 2009). Greenpeace, on the other hand, says that the oil companies support climate deniers because they want to go on making vast profits. Who are we to believe? A moment's thought would give you the answer—if you try to be "rational." (For more on the climate crisis, see Chapter 9.)

Thinking for ourselves—that's what Chomsky means by being "rational." It also means scrutinizing accepted beliefs and systems of authority: looking for evidence that supports them or challenges them, and drawing evidence-based conclusions. This leads us to our next topic: anarchism.

4. Anarchism

Any structure of power and authority needs to be challenged to justify itself. If—as is usually the case—it cannot be justified, it should be dismantled. (Chomsky 2014a: 116)

A narchism for Chomsky boils down to this attitude—skeptical, critical, challenging—rather than a comprehensive political philosophy. In fact, Chomsky has no time for comprehensive philosophies of any kind, because they are lazy and discourage people from thinking for themselves. He often says that any word ending in "-ism" should be distrusted, especially if it involves a person's name—for instance, *Marxism*, *Reaganism*, and *Thatcherism*. He also has no time for words beginning with *post-*, so *post-modernism* is doubly dubious for him. He says that explanations of post-modernism strike him as either incomprehensible or banal, whereas scientists who work in very difficult, specialized fields can usually explain to him their main ideas in a way he can understand.

The anarchist tradition

Anarchism is more than just a critical attitude, though. Chomsky often locates himself within a wider "left-libertarian tradition," which has a clear aim that he spells out in this passage, starting—again—with John Dewey:

> A more just and free society, a society in which, in [Dewey's] words, 'the ultimate aim of production is not production of goods, but the production of free human beings associated with one another on terms of equality.' This basic commitment, which runs through all of Dewey's work and

thought, is profoundly at odds with the two leading currents of modern social intellectual life; one, strong in his day–he was writing in the 1920s and 1930s about these things–is associated with the command economies in Eastern Europe, the systems created by Lenin and Trotsky and turned into an even greater monstrosity by Stalin. The other, the state capitalist industrial society being constructed in the U.S. and much of the West, with the effective rule of private power. These two systems are similar in some fundamental ways, including ideologically. Both were, and one of them remains, deeply authoritarian in fundamental commitment, and both were very sharply and dramatically opposed to another tradition, the Left libertarian tradition, with roots in Enlightenment values, a tradition that included progressive liberals of the John Dewey variety, independent socialists like Bertrand Russell, leading elements of the Marxist mainstream, mostly anti-Bolshevik, and of course libertarian socialists and various anarchist movements, not to speak of major parts of the labor movement and other popular sectors.

This independent Left, of which Dewey was a part, has strong roots in classical liberalism. It grows right out of it, in my opinion, and it stands in sharp opposition to the absolutist currents of state capitalist and state socialist institutions and thought. (Chomsky 2000b: 37-8)

In the UK, the "independent Left" tends to coalesce and be visible in periods of crisis, such as the disastrous and fraudulent invasion of Iraq in 2003. Opponents of the invasion included many members of the Liberal Party, the Left of the Labour Party (including the Foreign Secretary, Robin Cook, who resigned from the government during the build-up to the invasion), several trade unions, a number of far-left and Marxist organizations like the Socialist Workers Party, various peace groups, and a range of anarchist and libertarian socialist groups. There were many disagreements within this diverse alliance, but they have much in common.

Internationally, the Global Justice Movement (sometimes wrongly called the Anti-Globalisation Movement) that began in the late 1990s, the World Social Forum ("Another World is possible"), the Occupy movement, the Arab Spring, the Climate Strikes started by Greta Thunberg, and other worldwide initiatives all have substantial libertarian socialist ingredients. Organizations like ZNet, Truthout and Counterpunch in the US, Global Research in Canada, New Matilda in Australia, and Skwawkbox and Left Foot Forward in the UK can all be counted as part of the "independent Left," along with prominent campaigners such as Ralph Nader, Naomi Klein, George Monbiot, Rebecca Solnit, Bill McKibben, Owen Jones, Rachel Shabi and Milan Rai. Nonviolent protest has been a key element of all these movements.

People often ask Chomsky how they can join his "movement," and his typical answer is (a) he has no special advice to give, and it's a mistake to think he does; (b) there are lots of ways to change the world—you don't have to look hard to find them; and (c) go ahead and do it. He tells us to distrust famous people, including himself, and to think for ourselves. (But see Chapter 17 for some suggestions.)

Power in corporations and universities

An example of a "structure of power and authority," frequently challenged by Chomsky, is any business corporation—any company that sells products or services. He often uses the term "fascist" to describe how corporations are organized: he means that power percolates downwards within them, so that the people at the top have authority over the next layer of management, who in turn have power over the people under them, and so on down to the bottom of the organization—the people who do the lowest-paid jobs such as cleaning the toilets or making the tea and coffee. At each layer, the people who work in a corporation are accountable to their manager, who in turn is accountable to his or her manager, and so on upwards. Fear inevitably rules in such an organization, hence the term "fascist." (Chomsky also refers to corporations as "private tyrannies.") Good managers try to reduce fear and increase collaboration, but the structure often works against them. There are, of course, plenty of zombie managers, who implement the authoritarian system without thinking, and no shortage of thuggish managers who enjoy bullying their underlings. Big corporations, notably those dealing in fossil fuels, agriculture, and hi-tech, are currently engaged in destroying the planet in pursuit of short-term profit—see Chapter 9 for more about this topic.

Armed forces around the world are organized in this top-down way as well. Governments seem to need a group of people who will obey any instruction unthinkingly, including orders to endanger themselves and kill other people—though fighting wars is only a part of what soldiers can be ordered to do. Helping after natural disasters, for example, is generally a good thing. A soldier who refuses to obey an order can be severely punished, though, in extreme cases through murder by firing squad. The armed forces are notorious for breeding bullies and fostering massive corruption. Two examples: in the US, a 2010 Government Accountability Office (GAO) report found that the 98 ongoing Major Defense Acquisition Programs were collectively $402 billion over budget (Perlo-Freeman 2016). In 2014, a UK subsidiary of AgustaWestland was fined €300,000—and its parent company AgustaWestland was fined €80,000—to settle an Italian investigation into allegations of bribery relating to the sale of 12 helicopters to India's military. In addition, the court ordered the confiscation of €7.5 million in company profits. (Dixon et al. 2018) (See below for more about this delightful company.)

My personal experience, though less brutal, has been similar. I worked in a UK university that has a top-down management structure. In many UK universities, this means that the senior staff (the Vice-Chancellor, deputy VCs, Head of Human Resources, Head of Finance, and so on) are not accountable to academics like me or any other regular staff. The top people are appointed by a "Board of Governors," or a "University Council," which has very limited staff representation, and they appoint the ones below them, who appoint the ones below them. This kind of hierarchical organization generates bullying. People higher up tend to assume that people below them in the hierarchy, including teaching staff, are like naughty children, who need firm discipline or we would do little or no work.

Some universities in my country have limited democracy, where Heads of Department are elected by teaching staff and serve for a fixed period (after which they usually need time to recover from their battles on behalf of their colleagues and against the higher echelons). The two best-known British universities, Oxford and Cambridge, have even more democracy. In French universities, elections for Heads of Department, Deans, Vice-Chancellors (Présidents/Présidentes), and other senior posts are the norm. The French system is not perfect, partly because these elected people have to battle the Ministry of Education, but I am not aware of any catastrophic consequences that result from this democracy. One advantage is that there is less scope for anger about the large salaries that Vice-Chancellors earn (currently, and rightly, a *cause célèbre* in UK universities), because in France (a) their salaries are lower, (b) their positions are temporary, and (c) they are subject to removal if staff object to them.

Trade Unions are important in resisting fear-based management. Chomsky writes that the decline in union membership and influence in the US was a deliberate goal of corporations (2003: 13), because "unions [...] provide a stable and continuing basis for education and social and political action" (1987: 172).

Government power

Chomsky thinks some structures of power and authority can justify themselves, but that most cannot. As we saw in Chapter 2, he argues that decisions about investment, how work is organized, and many other parts of life, should be made democratically, not left in the hands of a few people—mostly men. Apart from the moral reasons for doing this, a system that encourages everyone to put forward ideas and plans is likely to be more adaptable and creative than one where decisions are taken by a few people at the top.

Anarchists often oppose "governments" and "the state." Chomsky's position is more nuanced. Today's large corporations are more powerful than many states, so governments, or groups of governments, can be a positive countervailing force against the corporations, which are not answerable to voters. We noted in Chapter 2 that he votes in elections when he thinks this will make a difference. Governments are, to some extent, accountable—if they are democratic, and if the democracy is not corrupted, as it is in many countries, by financial inducements and threats from corporations (see Chapter 10 for more about this).

In the UK, there is a "revolving door": a small group of wealthy people move between company boards, top civil service posts, and government positions. Patricia Hewitt, Minister of Health in the Labour Government from 2005 to 2007, became a special consultant to the world's largest pharmacy chain, Alliance Boots, in 2008. In the same year, she joined the British Telecom (BT) Group board as a non-executive director. Geoff Hoon, Labour Defence Secretary from 1999 to 2005 (a period that included the disastrous invasion of Iraq in 2003), is currently Managing Director of International Business at AgustaWestland, a company that manufactures military equipment and that made a profit of over four billion euros in 2012. The record of Conservative Party politicians is even more sleazy: two recent examples are Liam Fox, Minister of Defence from 2010 to 2011 and Secretary of State for International Trade from 2016 to 2019 (details in Egret 2017), and Priti Patel, International Development Secretary from 2016 to 2017 and Home Secretary (Interior Minister) at the time of writing (cf. Miller 2017).

Encouraging real democracy

Chomsky's advocacy of democracy, and his challenge to structures of power and authority, are based on the belief that human beings are naturally co-operative, compassionate, intelligent, and eager to engage in meaningful collaborative work over which they have control. Anarchism for him means working for a social order where these positive qualities are promoted and encouraged, and the negative parts of human nature are not. He emphasizes that these beliefs have no scientific basis. Basically, the choice is between optimism and despair, as the title of one of Chomsky's books puts it (Chomsky & Polychroniou, 2017). Optimism about human nature is more constructive, more empowering, and more fun.

Many people find it hard to think for themselves and to challenge "structures of power and authority." Why is this? A lot of work has been done by thoughtful and intelligent people to address this issue. In my opinion, the main reasons are the education system, which generally fosters fear and conformity (see Chapter 3), and propaganda by powerful elites—to which we now turn.

5. Propaganda

In our system what you might call "state propaganda" isn't expressed as such, as it would be in a totalitarian society—rather it's implicit, it's presupposed, it provides the framework for debate among the people who are admitted into mainstream discussion. (NC in Mitchell & Schoeffel 2002:13)

Between the mid-1960s and 1998, my country was involved in a civil war in which nearly 3,500 people died and many others were injured. Bombs killed civilians in Manchester, Omagh, and other towns and cities. Lives were wrecked, innocent people were tortured by the police, and some were wrongfully imprisoned for many years, most famously those who became known as the Guildford Four and the Birmingham Six.

Here are two notable events from that time.

In 1971, the British army took 14 men to a secret location in rural County Derry in Northern Ireland and subjected them to a horrific interrogation from which they have never recovered. According to Amnesty International:

> The men were forced to wear hoods and thrown to the ground from low-flying helicopters while hooded. [...] On top of brutal beatings and death threats, the men were then subjected to what would become known as the five techniques, authorized at a high level:

- Hooding
- Stress positions
- White noise
- Sleep deprivation
- Deprivation of food and water

None of the fourteen men were ever convicted of any criminal offense. (Amnesty International 2018)

The following year, British soldiers opened fire on a protest march in Derry, killing 14 people and injuring 14 more. A long-delayed government inquiry into the "Bloody Sunday" slaughter concluded in 2010 that "none of the victims had posed any threat to the soldiers and that their shooting was without justification" (Encyclopaedia Britannica 2019).

The civil war was a horrible period that corrupted British democracy and generated a climate of fear for much of my life. One of the achievements of Tony Blair's Labour government was the Good Friday Agreement of 1998, under which the British Army withdrew from Northern Ireland, violence almost ceased, and some astonishing reconciliation took place: to take one example, the firebrand Protestant cleric and Unionist politician Ian Paisley (he routinely denounced the Pope as "The Antichrist"), became a close friend of the leading Republican Martin McGuinness, a Catholic and former leading IRA commander. Chomsky has praised the agreement on many occasions, for instance:

> It is necessary to attend to the grievances that regularly lie in the background of terrorism, and when they are legitimate, remedy them—which should be done anyway. And it is necessary to convince the pool of potential recruits that there is a better course. That's the right approach if the aim is to reduce terrorism. And it works. Indonesia and Northern Ireland are good examples. (Chomsky 2010: 152)

I discussed the bias of the British media towards this civil war in my earlier book on Chomsky (Salkie 1990: 173-9). My concern now, however, is that the Good Friday Agreement is under severe threat. A key provision of the Agreement was an open border between Northern Ireland and the Republic of Ireland, replacing the armed fortresses which the British Army erected during the civil war, and which were prime targets of paramilitary attacks. If this "hard border" is reinstated, it will once again be widely hated, and almost certainly lead to more violence. Any rational person who lived through the civil war should be appalled at this prospect, and do their utmost to prevent it. If UK newspapers and TV had an ounce of courage and sense, they would be screaming every day about the need to keep an open border in Ireland. Pictures of bloodstained victims of the war would be on the front pages, with headlines asking "Do you want to return to this?" Commentators would be begging the government to avoid another civil war.

The issue is in the news, of course, but almost entirely as an annoying detail in the negotiations about the UK leaving the European Union—the so-called "Brexit." Political leaders in other EU countries, particularly the Republic of Ireland, recognize how important it is to preserve the Good Friday agreement. In the UK, the media marginalize the threat of another civil war and barely mention the horrors that lie ahead if a "hard border" is imposed in Ireland. As I write, the mainstream British media are obsessed with the UK and the European Union. Terms like "No Deal Brexit," "trade deals" and the like are on everyone's lips—everyone who matters, that is. There are fierce arguments between "leavers" and "remainers." The issue of preventing another civil war in the UK is there, but only barely.

Another example

Let's look at a similar situation in the US media. As I write, two territories have experienced recent huge protests against the regime that rules them. In Hong Kong, over a million people—about one-eighth of the population—have demonstrated for democracy and against China. In Puerto Rico, a US colony in the Caribbean, more than half a million—about one-sixth of the population—have protested against the Governor, Ricardo Rossello, and against the United States. One of these protest movements has been reported prominently in the US and UK media. The other one has barely been mentioned.[1]

Here is some background about Puerto Rico. A Spanish Colony for about 400 years, the island was taken over by the US in 1898. Writing in 1987, Chomsky summed up what happened next (at that time he devoted a lot of attention to Central and Southern America and the Caribbean):

> Puerto Rico [...] was turned into a sugar plantation for the benefit of U.S. agribusiness, virtually eliminating native agriculture. Later, an industrialization strategy based on tax exemptions and other incentives led to industrial growth for export. By Third World standards, Puerto Rico ranks high in terms of per capita income, life expectancy and the like. The other side of the coin is that 40% of the population have emigrated to urban slums in the United States (at a rate that reached its peak in the 1980s), farmlands are virtually abandoned, 60% of the population are dependent on food stamps and most of the rest work in foreign-owned factories or government offices supported by the U.S. government. Two-thirds of the adult population do not work at all [...]

'In short, the U.S. public underwrites the Puerto Rican people, while U.S. corporations shift profits through their Puerto Rican plants and back to the United States, tax free,' economist Richard Weisskoff observes in a recent study. This 'great industrial strength,' he adds, 'is based on a tax gimmick that is also subject to revision. Much of the economic survival of Puerto Rico is due to pecuniary advantages, to fiscal or international bookkeeping rules that, if changed, can bring on more hardship' to a 'bankrupt, dismembered economy heavily dependent on welfare.'

[...] the costs are social costs while the benefits are private benefits. The costs of the British Navy, or the U.S. military system, or food stamps to control popular dissidence in

Puerto Rico, and so on, are paid by the general population of the imperial society. The profits go to investors, exporters, banks, commercial institutions, agribusiness and the like. (Chomsky 1987: 74-5)

In September 2017, the island was devastated by a powerful hurricane, killing an estimated 3,000 people. Many of them could have been saved if they had had speedy access to medical care. It took a year to restore electricity (Weisbrot 2019). But Puerto Rico's problems had begun much earlier when the "international bookkeeping rules" and massive corruption led to the administration going bankrupt.

> Puerto Rico has a Financial Oversight and Management Board (FOMB), created by the US Congress and appointed by the president of the United States, in charge of its finances. Its budget, financed by Puerto Rico's taxpayers, is $1.5 billion over five years, or $300 million a year. [...] The vast majority of the FOMB's budget ($1.1 billion) goes to advisers and consultants. And there are serious potential conflicts of interest among the board itself. (Weisbrot 2019)

The hurricane was reported in the US media and across the world. But the financial chicanery that led to the mass protests has gone almost unreported. Instead, the coverage is about investment: a typical example is an article in the Business section of the *New York Times* headlined "$129 Billion Puerto Rico Bankruptcy Plan Could Be Model for States." The article outlines the plan "for resolving the biggest governmental bankruptcy in United States history," and discusses which investors will do best and which will lose out. Government employees, current and retired, will lose out, and pensions will become less generous (a familiar story in recent years, as workers pay for the financial crisis of 2008, I might add). The article notes that "The island's teachers rejected the plan in a preliminary vote," (*New York Times*, 2019).

If the media were genuinely independent, they would highlight and explain the threat of renewed civil war in Ireland and the scandal of the Puerto Rico debt crisis. Instead, they focus on trivial issues, such as the latest bizarre tweet by Donald Trump, or the personality of leading politicians in the UK. Personalities are news, policies generally aren't. If you believe the media, Trump definitely has a personality, but former UK Prime Minister Theresa May seemingly does not. So what?

One of the ways this works is by presenting political debate as a contest between different points of view, rather like a football game. There are winners and losers. Not long ago, the President of South Africa, Jacob Zuma, was forced to resign (loser), and the new President is Cyril Ramaphosa (winner). In press reports, the word "corruption" was routinely linked with Zuma. I learned nothing about his policies or those of his successor.

The Propaganda Model

During general elections, the reporting is even more vacuous. Since I was a child, I have found election media circuses an insult to my intelligence. It has always seemed to me that the wrong issues are debated in the wrong way. Why is this?

Chomsky has an answer which he calls the *Propaganda Model* (in fact, he says that his co-author Edward Herman should take much of the credit for their book, Herman & Chomsky, 1988, which introduced the model). He says that it is by far the best-supported theory in social science, that it is largely taken for granted by elite opinion, and that its basic premises are just common sense.

Here it is. The major media outlets are mostly part of huge corporations, with some exceptions. In the US, the National Public Radio (NPR) and Public Broadcasting System (PBS), are, as their names suggest, publicly-owned. In the UK, some of the main TV and radio channels are part of the British Broadcasting Corporation (BBC) and are publicly-owned as well. This means they have no advertisements, for which I thank the Lord regularly. But most of the media, like any corporation, need to sell a product to their customers and make a profit. The product is audiences and readers, and their customers are advertisers—usually other big corporations:

> The economic structure of a newspaper is that it sells readers to other businesses. See, they're not really trying to sell newspapers to people [...] So what they're doing is selling audiences to other businesses, and for the agenda-setting media like the New York Times and the Washington Post and the Wall Street Journal, they're in fact selling very privileged, elite audiences to other businesses—overwhelmingly their readers are members of the so-called 'political class,' which is the class that makes decisions in our society. (NC in Mitchell & Schoeffel 2002:14)

What would a rational person expect of the media in light of these simple facts? You would expect them to reflect the interests of their advertisers. It would be surprising if they didn't support the economic, social, and political agendas of big corporations. That isn't a "conspiracy theory," it's just an obvious truth.

The Propaganda Model says that the media do this by the way they select topics, set out the issues, filter information, and focus their analyses, as well as their emphasis and tone. An example is an article in the British Daily Mirror from March 2018 (Bartlett 2018). Its headline said that Jeremy Corbyn, the Labour Party leader, was "strengthening his hold on the Labour Party" when its General Secretary resigned. Instead of presenting Corbyn as hungry for power, we can imagine other ways of presenting this news: for example, as the democratically elected leader of the Party doing what he had been elected to do.

Similarly, when the Guardian wants a critical comment about the Conservative government, it mostly turns to someone from the small Liberal Democrat party, rather than a member of the opposition—the Labour Party. The choices that the newspaper makes are not the only possible ones, and they reflect a persistent partisanship against the left of the Labour Party. (Remember the choice between "sarcasm" and "humor" in Chapter 2.) The less liberal newspapers are more openly biased, but the bias is everywhere when you look for it. The BBC is not immune: many of its journalists move to and from privately-owned media, as well as corporate "Public Relations" jobs.

Testing the Model

You can test the Propaganda Model any day by picking a news story and imagining other ways in which it could have been written, starting with the headline. You can also ask why it was chosen as news in the first place. (These are the basic principles of *Critical Discourse Analysis*, unfortunately often submerged under a mountain of unhelpful jargon. An exception, highly recommended, is Richardson 2007.) Next time you read a report about "the immigration problem," imagine how a refugee or migrant would have written it. Look at which countries feature in the news and which do not. For US readers, nothing of any interest apparently happens in Mauritania, Guatemala, Senegal, Paraguay, Mozambique, Djibouti, or Kazakhstan, except possibly natural disasters.

According to the Propaganda Model, there is no reason to expect that the media will always support government policy. Different parts of the business elite control the government from time to time: sometimes it is traditional manufacturing that has most influence, sometimes banks and the financial sector, sometimes hi-tech companies. There are often tactical disagreements between these different sectors. The Propaganda Model predicts that the entire range of elite opinion will be found in the media—but very few opinions that go beyond that. The more vigorous the debate—as with the personalities of political leaders—the more effectively the hidden shared assumptions are taken for granted and strengthened. (For some useful discussion, search on the web for Overton

Window, a term sometimes used for the acceptable limits of political debate.)

"We are not biased or censored"

Many journalists have responded to these claims with outrage. They say that no one interferes with their news reports or tells them what to write about and how to write about it. That misses the point. The values of the elite are so deeply ingrained that journalists adopt them unthinkingly. If they didn't do that, they wouldn't be in their jobs. There is occasional planned interference—the *Guardian* interviews with Chomsky mentioned in Chapter 2 are an example—but mostly interference and censorship are not necessary because journalists know which lines they cannot cross. Chomsky and Herman call this "brainwashing under freedom," and it is a much more effective system than state propaganda because it is unstated and taken for granted.

A comment on Chomsky's supposed "anti-Americanism" (cf. Myth 5 in chapter 2) is relevant here. Chomsky often says that the United States is an extraordinarily free society, where dissidents like him are marginalized but rarely imprisoned, tortured, or murdered by death squads as in many other countries. People with opinions outside the mainstream can find themselves unemployed and suffering financially—a serious deterrent to independent thinking—but are seldom arrested because of their views. In a country where the rich and powerful have limited power to use violence or the threat of violence against opposition voices, propaganda is likely to be especially important. Hence the unusual pro-business dominance of the media in the US and the lack of a mainstream political party that is explicitly social-democratic, let alone "socialist." Let's not forget the comparatively enormous power of organized Christianity (compared, for instance, to European countries), and the huge emphasis on mainstream culture (TV, films, music, sport, etc.). Of course, the latter are also promoted massively around the world.

Herman and Chomsky tested their model of how the media work on many detailed examples. They compared media coverage of atrocities committed by enemy states (at the time, the Soviet Union and the Eastern European countries) with coverage of similar cruelties for which the US and its allies were responsible. They contrasted reports of elections in enemy states and in client states. In every case, the model was confirmed.

The Propaganda Model makes one particularly striking prediction. It expects that it will be ignored and misrepresented in mainstream culture—in fact, that it will not even be understandable to elites, no matter how strongly the evidence supports it. Because it challenges important institutions and the ideologies that underpin them, it is troublesome to them and will be excluded. That's exactly what has happened.

And the conformism and subservience to power fostered by the education system (cf. Chapter 3) are all part of "brainwashing under freedom."

6. Korea

On 27 April 2018, the two Koreas signed a historic declaration
in which they "affirmed the principle of determining the
destiny of the Korean nation on their own accord." [...] The
declaration was virtually a plea to outsiders (meaning the
US) not to interfere with these efforts. To Trump's credit, he
has not undermined these efforts—and has been bitterly
condemned across the spectrum for his sensible stand.
(Chomsky 2019: 25-6)

K orea is about 7,500 miles from Washington, DC. The Korean
peninsula is slightly larger than the state of Indiana—one third
the size of France—and it has not attacked any of its neighbors
recently—unlike Japan, which held Korea as a colony from 1910 to
1945. Between 1950 and 1953, the United States and its allies fought
a hugely destructive war against the northern part of Korea. Sad to
say, tensions have continued in the intervening 66 years. The "Foal
Eagle" military exercises, conducted by South Korean and US forces
from 1997 to 2017, were probably the largest in the world. What is
this all about? Why is Korea still in the headlines? And for heaven's
sake, how can Chomsky call President Trump's policy on Korea
"sensible?"

In fact, the story of Korea is a good way to understand the history
of the world since 1945. At the end of WWII, most of Europe was
in ruins, and this was even truer for much of East Asia. Japan was,
of course, utterly devastated: 60 cities were more than 40 percent
destroyed, on average, by conventional bombing, and two cities
were flattened by atomic bombs in August 1945. It is not widely
known that Hiroshima and Nagasaki were chosen because few other
targets remained. Tokyo, for instance, had already been laid waste
by massive conventional bombing raids. (cf. Chomsky 1969a: 170)
One such raid on Tokyo in March 1945 killed at least 80,000 people

and destroyed over a quarter of a million buildings (Lee 2015: 72). Chomsky comments:

> If you look at the U.S. Strategic Bombing Survey after the war, it points out that more people were killed during [the Tokyo] bombing in a six-hour period than ever in human history. (Chomsky 1996:60)

This was the high point of US supremacy–military and economic. The British Empire, which had once controlled about a quarter of the world economy, was in decline, and the US now accounted for about half of global output. US strategic planners had two priorities. The first was to gain control of as much of the world's oil supply as possible, the great majority of it in the Middle East. The second was to keep control of other raw materials and of the markets. Internal US government planning documents, often cited by Chomsky, make these two priorities clear.[1]

Threats to US control

We will focus on oil in the next chapter. The main threat to the second type of control was independent nationalist movements around the world, which naturally wanted to have some say in how their own countries were run. These movements usually wanted to take back their land, industry, and financial system from the UK and the US, as well as from the local elites who were part of the colonial system. Much of post-war history only makes sense as part of the clash between nationalist and anti-colonial movements around the world on one hand, and the UK, the US, and other colonial powers such as France and the Netherlands on the other.

Some of the most important conflicts were in India (including present-day Pakistan and Bangladesh) against the UK; Algeria against France; and Vietnam against France and then the US.

Korea fits into this picture perfectly. After the defeat of Japan in World War II, Korea was divided along the 38th Parallel, with the north under Soviet occupation and the south under US control. During Japanese rule, local resistance to the occupation had grown, and by 1945 the Koreans had set up functioning local administration over much of the country. According to Chomsky, the US dismantled all of that by force, using Koreans who had collaborated with the Japanese, and even re-instituting the Japanese police too. (NC in Mitchell & Schoeffel 2002: 302) Similar stories could be told about post-1945 Germany, France, Greece, and Italy. Chomsky often refers to how the US recruited Nazi war criminals such as Reinhard Gehlen: he had headed Germany's military intelligence on the Eastern Front during the war, and was given the same duties in the new West German State under close CIA supervision (cf. Chomsky 1987: 31; 1989: 27). On American subversion of democracy in postwar France, Greece, and Italy, see NC in Mitchell & Schoeffel (2002: 160-163).

The Korean War

For several years after 1945, there was a bitter civil war in the south of Korea, with about 100,000 people killed, including 30,000-60,000 slaughtered in the suppression of a peasant insurgency on Cheju (Jeju) Island in 1948 (Chomsky 1987: 29). Meanwhile, in the north, former national resistance leaders had continued to flourish. After a lull in the civil war, forces from the north invaded the south in 1950. The US and its allies sent in armed forces to oppose the northern army, and over a million people died in what is now called "The Korean War." This phase ended with an armistice agreement in 1953, intended to end hostilities between the two sides and safeguard peace on the peninsula.

The brutality of the US military was staggering. A leading historian of the Korean War writes:

The United States dropped 635,000 tons of bombs in Korea (not counting 32,557 tons of napalm), compared to 503,000 tons in the entire Pacific theater in World War II. [...] Estimates of the destruction of towns and cities in North Korea ranged from forty to ninety percent; at least 50 percent of eighteen out of the North's twenty-two major cities were obliterated. (Cumings 2010: 159)

Chomsky comments:

Towards the end of what we call the "Korean War" [...] the United States ran out of good bombing targets. We had total command of the air of course, but there was nothing good left to bomb–because everything had already been flattened. So we started going after things like dikes. Okay, that's just a major war crime. In fact, if you take a look at the official U.S. Air Force history of the Korean War, it's absolutely mind-boggling, it's like something straight out of the Nazi archives. I mean, these guys don't conceal their glee at all, it's just this account of all their terrific feelings: we bombed these dikes, and a huge flow of water went through the valleys and carved out huge paths of destruction and slaughtered people! And they say, laughingly: we don't realize how important rice is for the Asians, so naturally they were screaming with rage! (NC in Mitchell & Schoeffel 2002: 302)

After the armistice

After the 1953 armistice, the US continued to arm the Republic of Korea (ROK, South Korea) and threaten the Democratic People's Republic of Korea (DPRK, North Korea). This has continued until the present day, including the "Foal Eagle" military exercises mentioned earlier. Meanwhile, in the DPRK, the armed forces were also built up, including nuclear weapons. Contrary to most media reports, Chomsky argues that these are not the main threat to the ROK: the real menace is the massed DPRK artillery near the Demilitarized Zone–a strip of land that separates the two countries. The big guns are aimed at Seoul, the capital of South Korea, and the many US troops at the border (Chomsky 2005b: 50).

However, it has surely not escaped the attention of North Korean military planners that Iraq, Afghanistan, Serbia, and Libya–all heavily bombed by the US in recent times–did not have nuclear weapons. We don't have to like the fact that North Korea is developing nuclear weapons, but it is understandable. Chomsky says:

> Look, nobody in their right mind would want North Korea to have nuclear weapons. But on the other hand, there's nothing much that they would *do* with nuclear weapons if they had them, except maybe defend themselves from attack. They're certainly not going to *invade* anybody, that's not even imaginable: if they ever made a move, the country gets destroyed tomorrow. So the only role that nuclear weapons could play for them is as a deterrent to attack–and that's not totally unrealistic. (NC in Mitchell & Schoeffel 2002: 302)

The DPRK has become a repressive, inward-looking society. However, any country devastated by bombs, and then threatened for decades by the most powerful country in the world, would be likely to put an emphasis on security at the expense of democracy. US policy towards the DPRK has been driven–or so I claimed above–by a fear of national movements, independent of the US, succeeding. The DPRK has retained its independence, but its understandable preoccupation with security means that it has utterly failed to be a model for the rest of the world. To that extent, US policy has succeeded.

The current situation

Turning to the present day, tensions between the ROK and the DPRK are reducing as I write, with some (mostly symbolic) reduction in military installations, along with more frequent family visits, sports links, and so on. Unfortunately, we have seen this before, as Chomsky points out:

> In September 2005, a very far-reaching agreement was made in which North Korea committed to dismantling its nuclear weapons programs completely, and in return, the United States would terminate hostile gestures and threats, would provide a light-water reactor, as had been promised years earlier, and would move toward normalization of relations with North Korea. If that had been implemented, there wouldn't have been a North Korean bomb test, there wouldn't have been the current conflict, which is always verging on the edge of nuclear war. What happened then in September 2005? A few days after the agreement, the United States forced banks to freeze North Korean assets to cut them off from the world and in effect terminated the consortium that was talking about the light-water reactor.
> (Chomsky & Barsamian 2007: 48)

Current reporting in the mainstream media focuses on the North Korean nuclear weapons program; less biased reporting uses the term "denuclearization of the Korean peninsula," which the DPRK has repeatedly proposed and the United States has consistently rejected. (Similarly, mainstream reports about Iran talk about the alleged Iranian nuclear weapons program, but more honest reporting uses the term "denuclearization of the Middle East," regularly proposed by Iran but never accepted by the US. This is because it would involve the US officially admitting that Israel has nuclear weapons and negotiating to remove them). If the US were to stop interfering in Korea and let the ROK and the DPRK negotiate, progress might well be possible (as in the quote at the start of this chapter), but that is unlikely to happen: the huge US military presence in the region is no doubt intended mainly as a threat to China and Russia.

The South Korean story

The ROK is in many respects an economic success, unlike its northern counterpart. Chomsky often points out that the main reason for this has been the country's rejection of the economic model of "free markets." This is the model that the United States and the international financial institutions, mostly dominated by the US—the World Bank, the International Monetary Fund (IMF), and the World Trade Organization—have tried to force on developing countries, with disastrous consequences. To take just one illustration, the "Structural Adjustment Programmes" imposed on poor countries from the 1980s included a requirement that school fees had to be obligatory. How this could possibly have helped the many poor people in Zimbabwe or Pakistan is a mystery. A 2008 study by researchers at Cambridge and Yale universities found that IMF requirements for reduced spending on healthcare correlated systematically with an increase in tuberculosis in many countries in Eastern Europe (Stuckler et al. 2008).

Two final remarks about the ROK, rarely mentioned in the mainstream media: firstly, the economy has long been controlled by a small number of families. They own most of the country's large companies, known as the Chaebol, including Samsung, Hyundai, and LG (see Tejada 2017 for a discussion). This is a feature of many countries allied to the United States, notably Saudi Arabia, Cuba before 1959, and Venezuela until 1999. Secondly, the country has hardly been a beacon of stable democracy. Park Chung-hee came to power in a military coup in 1961 and ruled the country until he was assassinated in 1979. In that year, another coup by Chun Doo-hwan led to eight more years of military rule. Kim Dae-jung, the first genuinely democratic president of the ROK from 1998 to 2003, had previously been sentenced to death (later commuted), exiled, and imprisoned as an opposition activist: he was frequently compared to Nelson Mandela.

We can learn a lot from looking at Korea with Chomsky as a guide.

7. The Middle East

> The principle is quite clear: there has to be some settlement that recognizes the right of self-determination of Jews in something like the state of Israel, and the right of self-determination of Palestinians in something like a Palestinian state. And everybody knows where that Palestinian state would be—in the West Bank and Gaza Strip, along roughly the borders that existed before the Six Day War in 1967. [...]
>
> All of this has been obvious for years—why hasn't it happened? Well, of course Israel's opposed to it. But the main reason it hasn't happened is because the United States has blocked it: the United States has been blocking the peace process in the Middle East for the last twenty years—we're the leaders of the rejectionist camp, not the Arabs or anybody else. (NC in Mitchell & Schoeffel 2002: 125)

Which Middle-Eastern country is the most important ally for the United States? Israel? Not according to Chomsky. In the words of a popular poster in 2003, the year of the US-led invasion of Iraq, "It's the oil, stupid." Most of the world's oil reserves are in Iran, Iraq, and the countries of the Arabian peninsula, with Saudi Arabia having by far the most. A State Department document of 1945, often quoted by Chomsky, describes Saudi oil as "a stupendous source of strategic power, and one of the greatest material prizes in world history" (e.g., Chomsky 1982: 310-11). A central feature of US policy has been to keep the oil under US control.

The main threat to that control has been the local population in the region, who had the bizarre idea that they had some rights over the country's resources. As we noted in the last chapter, crushing this type of local nationalism has long been a central driver in US foreign policy. Let's look at the three main oil-exporting countries in turn. Don't worry—we'll get to Israel and Palestine soon.

Saudi Arabia

The Kingdom of Saudi Arabia is an absolute monarchy, established in 1932 with British support. The regime has been ruthless in crushing all opposition. Hundreds of members of the royal family share political and economic power. After 1945, the US gradually replaced the UK as the King's most important ally. The US and the UK have sold huge amounts of weapons to the Saudi regime and have encouraged the Saudi ruling elite to spend or invest their billions in these two countries. The regime regularly imprisons, tortures, and executes citizens who oppose it, and call for democracy or equal rights for women. As a deterrent to all forms of dissent, authorities sometimes display in public the severed heads of those who were executed—a practice known as "crucifixion." Saudi money has also financed a large network of schools around the world that promote Wahabi Islam—an ultra-conservative doctrine.

Iran

The US and the UK organized a coup in Iran in 1953 which ousted Mohammad Mosaddegh, the moderate social democrat Prime Minister and handed power to the Shah (King), who became one of the world's most brutal dictators but was a reliable ally of the US. When the Shah too was ousted—this time by a popular uprising in 1979—the US (and Saudi Arabia) gave moral and military support to the similarly unpleasant regime in Iraq. During the eight-year-long war between Iraq and Iran in the 1980s, Iraq received massive support from the US, including help to develop and use chemical weapons. Iran continues to be threatened by the US to this day.

Iraq

In Iraq, Saddam Hussein, the country's ruthless dictator, moved away from his alliance with the US after the war with Iran and paid the price: a brief invasion in 1991, a no-fly policy, vicious sanctions during the following decade, and then a complete invasion in 2003, as the US tried to gain control of the country. The result was predictable: chaos and destruction throughout the region, the growth of fanatical armed militias, Kurdish control over much of the north of the country (mostly a good thing), and an increase in the political and military power of Iran in the region.

What about Israel?

So the main issue in the Middle East is the control of Saudi, Iraqi, and Iranian oil. Where does Israel fit in? Basically, the country has become a crucial strategic ally of the relentless US struggle to maintain its influence in the region and to crush local nationalism. The relationship took some time to develop fully, but the 1967 "Six Day War" between Israel and its neighbors–Egypt, Syria, and Jordan–was a major turning point. At that time, the US assault on the countries of Indochina was at its height, and the determined resistance of the National Liberation Front in South Vietnam was becoming a nightmare for elites in Washington. When Israel won a quick and devastating victory in 1967, powerful circles in the US were impressed by the ability of a colonial regime like Israel to show the Arabs who was in control. Chomsky writes:

From the late 1950s, [...] the U.S. government increasingly

came to accept the Israeli thesis that a powerful Israel is a "strategic asset" for the United States, serving as a barrier against indigenous radical nationalist threats to American interests [...]. Through the 1960s, American intelligence regarded Israel as a barrier to Nasserite pressure on the Gulf oil-producing states [...]. This conclusion was reinforced by Israel's smashing victory in 1967, when Israel quickly conquered the Sinai, Gaza, the West Bank and the Golan Heights [...]. In the 1970s, U.S. Analysts argued that Israel and Iran under the Shah served to protect U.S. Control over the oil-producing regions of the Gulf. After the fall of the Shah, Israel's role as a Middle East Sparta in the service of American power has evoked increasing American support. (Chomsky 1999a: 20-1)

Some history is useful here. Present-day Israel and many of its neighbors were part of the Ottoman (Turkish) Empire for four centuries until World War I. The empire was then dismantled by the victorious powers, Britain and France, and in 1922 the League of Nations gave the UK a "mandate" to run Palestine. Palestine had a Muslim majority until 1948, when Palestinian Jews created a Jewish state called Israel, and many of the Muslims were expelled from the land. Population estimates vary, but Jews are thought to have been a small minority in 1800—about 5,000 people or 2 percent of the population. By 1900, the proportion of Jews had risen to about 15 percent. Most of the increase was due to immigration from Russia and Eastern Europe, where Jews were subject to terrible mistreatment. A movement called "Zionism," which arose at the beginning of the 20th century, encouraged Jews from around the world to move to Palestine. By 1947, the proportion of Jews was about 30 percent. The new arrivals were driven from Europe by the Nazi persecution, as well as the discrimination they were subjected to in their native countries.

Since 1948, the status of Israel has been controversial, to say the least. There have been several wars between Israel and neighboring countries, and Palestinians who were expelled in 1948 and afterward have insisted on their right to return to their former homes. The conflict between Israel and the Palestinians has regularly turned violent and has threatened to spread more widely. If it does spill over to other regions, the danger of nuclear war remains—an important issue to which Chomsky has devoted a lot of attention.

Israel has become the main police force ("Sparta," as Chomsky put it) for the United States in the Middle East. It has received huge amounts of arms from the US. For anyone who knows the history of the Jews, this is a familiar story. There have been Jewish communities in Europe, Asia, and Africa for centuries, living as vulnerable minorities in different countries. Sometimes they were tolerated, but antisemitism persisted even then. A pattern emerged in which Jews were used by ruling elites as the visible face of the rulers: some prominent Jews were court favorites, tax collectors, or bankers. In turbulent times, antisemitism was whipped up by the rulers to deflect popular anger away from them and towards the Jews. Jews were regularly attacked, murdered or expelled—from England in 1290, and from Spain in 1492, to give just two examples.

The role of Israel in the Middle East is the modern equivalent of the historic role of Jews: when Arab elites are threatened, they can turn popular anger away from themselves toward Israel. The arrangement has worked in Israel's favor up to now, but it is a risky situation. If the United States decides to drop Israel as its strategic ally, the country's ability to defend itself will diminish dramatically—just as in the past, rulers have supported Jews when it suited them, but abandoned Jews when it didn't. That's why Chomsky describes Israel's strategy as dangerous and possibly suicidal.

So how can this problem be resolved? Actually, the Israel-Palestine conflict has a simple solution, one that has been proposed by the overwhelming majority of UN members since the 1970s, including the Arab countries and the Palestinians: Israel needs to withdraw its military forces and settlements from the remaining territories that it has occupied since 1967—the West Bank and the

Golan Heights. (It has already relinquished the Sinai peninsula and the Gaza Strip, though it continues to strangle Gaza). The Palestinians need their own state in the West Bank and Gaza, and there must be a solution to the problem of Palestinian refugees (not impossible, by the way—the number of refugees who would actually want to return is relatively small). Jerusalem should be an international city, jointly run by Israel and the Palestinians. Israel and its neighboring countries need security guarantees, and Israel should decommission its nuclear weapons.

All this would be the first step towards normal relations between Israel and its neighbors. What would happen then is speculative, but as normal trade and diplomatic relations develop in the region, it is likely that tensions would decrease, and Israelis and Palestinians could collaborate where it is in their joint interest: for example, over water, agriculture, other infrastructure, and general economic development.

Why has this not happened? The simple answer, according to Chomsky, is that the United States has consistently rejected it, with Israel—completely dependent on its master—doing the same. As long as the US uses Israel as its local police force, the solution remains out of reach. The basic problem is not Israeli intransigence, in Chomsky's view, but US strategic priorities. That's why he disagrees with people who say that the "Jewish Lobby" in America dictates US policy. He says it is fanciful to think a small number of American Jews have this kind of influence. The rich and powerful in the United States mostly support US foreign policy (after all, they are the ones who control it—see the first truism under Myth 1 in Chapter 2). Huge arms companies like Lockheed Martin make a lot of profit when the US government pays for arms exports to Israel.

Chomsky has also been skeptical about campaigns to isolate Israel, such as the BDS (Boycott, Disinvestment, Sanctions) movement. The real target of BDS should be the United States, he has said. Israel's brutal attacks on Palestinians and neighboring countries are an inevitable result, he argues, of the strategic alliance between Israel and the US. The growth of anti-Arab racism and crude nationalism in Israel, and the withering of the socialist principles which motivated some of its founders, were also entirely predictable. Recently, however, he has stated that he "strongly supports" BDS despite some "tactical differences" with the campaign (BDS 2017).

When the US stops trying to control the rest of the world, the problems in the Middle East will be solvable. Until then, the conflicts, and the risk of nuclear holocaust, will continue.

8. Nuclear Dangers

In the case of nuclear weapons, at least we know in principle how to overcome the threat of apocalypse: eliminate them.
(Chomsky 2014b)

In August 1965, a fire in a nuclear missile silo in Arkansas killed 53 people. A welder accidentally broke a fuel pipe, causing the spray of fuel to catch fire. The temperature in the launch duct rose nearly high enough to make part of the missile explode.

In January 1978, an oxidizer leak in a nearby nuclear missile silo, also in Arkansas, sent a 3,000-foot-long, 300-foot-wide, and 100-foot-high cloud of toxic fumes drifting across the U.S. Highway 65.

In September 1980, the missile that had been in the 1965 silo exploded in the 1978 silo. A maintenance worker had dropped a socket from a socket wrench down an 80-foot shaft, puncturing a fuel tank on the missile. An Air Force serviceman was killed, and the complex was destroyed. The missile was armed with a W-53 thermonuclear warhead, at that time the most powerful weapon ever carried by an American missile. The warhead had a yield of nine megatons–about three times the power of all the bombs dropped during World War II, including both atomic bombs. Mercifully, the warhead did not explode (cf. Karlin 2017).

That was close.

One man saved the world

In September 1983, the Soviet nuclear early warning system reported that up to six missiles had been fired from the United States. Lieutenant-Colonel Stanislav Petrov (1939–2017) was the duty officer that day, and he decided that the reports were a false alarm. Instead of retaliating with nuclear missiles against the US, he disobeyed orders and did not initiate a counterattack. Because of his good sense, you and I are alive today (cf. Chomsky 2015b: xiv).

That was even closer.

We have been fortunate so far. Unless we do something about nuclear weapons, our good fortune is likely to run out sooner or later. Chomsky quotes the former commander of the Strategic Air Command, General Lee Butler: he said that humanity has so far survived the nuclear age "by some combination of skill, luck, and divine intervention, and I suspect the latter in greatest proportion." (Chomsky 2014b)

Nuclear warheads

There are currently around 13,400 nuclear warheads in the world: about 6,000 each in the US and Russia, and the remainder in France (290), China (320), the UK (210), India (about 150), Pakistan (the same), Israel (about 90) and North Korea (30-40) (Source: ICAN, 2019).

During the Cuban Missile Crisis of 1962, liberal US President John F. Kennedy brought the world to the brink of destruction with his insistence that the United States had the right to position nuclear weapons near the Soviet border, but the Soviet Union did not have the same right with respect to the US. Chomsky points out that Robert McNamara, Kennedy's Defense Secretary at the time, said that the world "came within a hair's breadth of nuclear disaster." Writing in 2005, McNamara described "current U.S. nuclear weapons policy as immoral, illegal, militarily unnecessary and dreadfully dangerous," creating "unacceptable risks to other nations and to our own" (Chomsky 2008: 138-9).

In a rare outburst of good sense, 190 states signed the Nuclear Non-Proliferation Treaty (NPT) in 1968. Its aim was to prevent the spread of nuclear weapons and to encourage countries that have weapons to get rid of them. These nations–at the time, the US, the Soviet Union, the UK, France, and China–pledged to make "good faith" efforts to eliminate them. None of them have. Recent US Presidents have repeatedly modernized their nuclear arsenal, and the current UK government is committed to spending billions on upgrading the country's Trident nuclear submarine fleet. When less stupid people call for nuclear disarmament, they are routinely dismissed as hopelessly naïve.

The cost and the danger

It is worth emphasizing how much nuclear weapons cost. The International Campaign against Nuclear Weapons (ICAN), which received the Nobel Peace Prize in 2017, says that countries that have nuclear weapons spend more than $300 million a day–well over $105 billion a year–on nuclear weapons. The British Trident submarines have cost about 5 percent of the country's defense budget since they were introduced in 1994. Nuclear armaments (and, incidentally, nuclear power stations) are phenomenally expensive: they involve a massive transfer of money from taxpayers to the military and private companies that manufacture them (on corruption and waste in the arms industry, see Chapter 4).

The Bulletin of the Atomic Scientists is an international association of leading scientific experts, including the British Astronomer Martin Rees, former President of the Royal Society. Every year, the Association updates the Doomsday Clock, an estimate of how close we are to the nuclear apocalypse–unless, of course, we eliminate nuclear weapons altogether. (See Bulletin of the Atomic Scientists 2019). In 1995, the clock was set at 14 minutes to midnight: by 2018 it was two minutes, and now it is 100 seconds. (The clock includes the growing danger of Climate Catastrophe–see the next chapter.)

What can be done?

If you think that this nuclear proliferation is an acceptable state of affairs, then nothing I say is likely to convince you otherwise. Any rational person will agree: it is stupid to risk the end of human life in this way. Worryingly, the decisions that led us here have been taken calmly by men (almost no women) in offices around the world, not evil monsters foaming at the mouth. But Chomsky has been warning for many years that we have to do something about nuclear weapons.

What can we do?

Chomsky has a few suggestions. Firstly, we must put pressure on the nuclear powers to fulfill their obligations under the NPT. Countries such as India, Pakistan, and Israel which have not ratified the NPT must be encouraged (or pressured) to take steps to eliminate their weapons. The United Nations has proposed that all production of weapons-usable fissile materials should be restricted to an international agency, to which countries can apply for nonmilitary uses.

Secondly, we should establish more nuclear-weapons-free zones (NWFZs). Chomsky notes that a number of such zones already exist, for example in Africa, the South Pacific, and Southeast Asia. In April 1991, the U.N. Security Council affirmed: "The goal of establishing in the Middle East a zone free from weapons of mass destruction and all missiles for their delivery and the objective of a global ban on chemical weapons" (Resolution 687, Article 14). Chomsky notes that the goal of a Middle East nuclear-weapons-free zone "has been endorsed by Iran, and is supported by a large majority of Americans and Iranians. It is, however, dismissed by the U.S. government and both political parties, and is virtually unmentionable in mainstream discussion" (Chomsky 2012: 28).

Thirdly, we must try to resolve conflicts and reduce the risk of nuclear weapons actually being used.

The United Nations has resolved repeatedly and overwhelmingly to pursue the first two of these proposals, and the very existence of the UN is devoted to the third. These are not impossible goals. We have the power to remove the shadow of nuclear catastrophe from the world forever. It would be utterly idiotic not to do so.

9. Climate Catastrophe

A short conversation about the climate crisis

Dramatis Personae (Sorry about the Latin, but that's what we playwrights say)

C = Chomsky (all genuine quotes).

S = Scientist, loosely based on Susan Solomon, Professor of Environmental Studies at MIT. (All genuine quotes, some lightly edited, from MIT Center for Global Change Science).

A = Alex, a typical American, based on opinion surveys.

R = Guess who! He likes to stir things up.

C: In 2006, 86 percent of [US] respondents favored requiring utilities, or encouraging them with tax breaks, to reduce the amount of greenhouse gases they emit ... Also in that year, 87 percent favored tax breaks for utilities that produce more electricity from water, wind, or sunlight ... (Chomsky 2015a: 141)

A: I am part of that majority. I cycle, recycle, and have a reusable coffee cup. I buy mostly organic vegetables. I would replace my gas-fueled car with an electric car if I could afford it. I want my grandchildren to have clean air and water. I don't want the Antarctic ice sheet to melt, though I won't weep many tears if Miami disappears.

R: That's great, unless you live in Miami. Now put the fear of God into Alex, Noam.

C: Those actions are important, but they're nowhere near what needs to be done. The threat is far greater than reported. The scientific literature describes a pace of destruction that is already frightening, and that might at any moment become nonlinear, abruptly rising far more sharply. Even without that, even with just the regular processes that are predicted, there is likely to be a rise in sea level in the not very distant future. This could be massively destructive to countries like Bangladesh, with its coastal plains, and cities like Boston, a good part of which could wind up under water. (Chomsky & Barsamian 2017)

The Himalayan glaciers are melting–that's the water supply for India and Pakistan. Already it's reported that there are about seventy-five million people in India who don't have access to clean drinking water. What's going to happen when this number increases? One very likely scenario is conflict between India and Pakistan over diminishing water supplies on which both of them rely. These are nuclear weapons states. They're already virtually at war. Suppose a water war breaks out? It will turn into a nuclear war very quickly ... (Chomsky & Barsamian 2017)

R: More please.

C: One might even take the speech President Barack Obama gave two years ago in the oil town of Cushing, Oklahoma, to be an eloquent death-knell for the species.

He proclaimed with pride, to ample applause, that 'Now, under my administration, America is producing more oil today than at any time in the last eight years. That's important to know. Over the last three years, I've directed my administration to open up millions of acres for gas and oil exploration across 23 different states. We're opening up more than 75 percent of our potential oil resources offshore. We've quadrupled the number of operating rigs to a record high. We've added enough new oil and gas pipeline to encircle the Earth and then some.' (Chomsky 2014b)

R: How about you, Susan? Can you frighten us too?

S: The most comprehensive modeling yet carried out on the likelihood of how much hotter the Earth's climate will get in this century shows that without rapid and massive action, the problem will be about twice as severe as previously estimated six years ago–and could be even worse than that. (Chandler 2009).

R: Any more nasty surprises?

S: Sure. At least half of the [past] sea level rise through thermal expansion due to increases in methane is expected to remain present for more than 200 years, even if anthropogenic emissions cease altogether. (Zickfield et al. 2017)

A: Terrifying. But what can I do?

C: Some of the things that can be done to counter climate change are elementary. Take weatherization–making energy-efficient homes. Not only would it delay the environmental crisis, it would help overcome the employment crisis. (Chomsky & Barsamian 2017)

Another example, which is kind of a scandal in the United States–if any of you have traveled abroad, you're perfectly aware of it–when you come back from almost anywhere in the world to the United States, it looks like you're coming to a Third World country, literally. The infrastructure is collapsing, transportation doesn't work. [... There] was a very systematic effort to redesign the society so as to maximize the use of fossil fuels. (Chomsky 2015a: 134-5)

Another component of any reasonable approach–and everyone on paper agrees with this–is to develop sustainable energy, green technology. We all know and everyone talks a nice line about that. (Chomsky 2015a: 136)

A: I would vote for all of those.

R: Assuming that you bother to vote at all. Between 1992 and 2016, voting turnout in US presidential elections ranged from 49% of eligible voters to just over 58%. That is far lower than in comparable wealthy democracies. It suggests that US democracy has major problems–see the next chapter!

C: The fact that the public is influenced by science [i.e. the figures in C's first contribution above–RS] is deeply troubling to those who dominate the economy and state policy. The American Legislative Exchange Council, ALEC, [is] a corporate-funded lobby that designs legislation to serve the needs of the corporate sector and extreme wealth. The Heartland Institute [is] a corporate-funded think tank dedicated to rejecting the scientific consensus on the climate. The Heartland Institute and ALEC are part of a huge campaign by corporate lobbies to sow doubt about the near-unanimous consensus of scientists that human activities are having a major impact on global warming with possibly ominous implications. ALEC and its corporate backers want the country to be "the stupid nation." (Chomsky 2015a: 141)

A: OK, I'm torn. I agree that there's a climate crisis right now, and that it's going to get worse. But how can I make a difference? The problems are so big and so frightening: they are paralyzing me. And the thought of taking on the corporate sector and extreme wealth makes it all sound impossible. We have a thuggish clown in the White House, and the Democrats talk good sometimes but look at Obama's record on fossil fuels. It's hopeless.

All the characters leave the stage, pursued by a bear. And most of the world's population disappear with them soon afterwards.

Action

Alex is exactly the kind of person that climate activists need to reach. S/he needs to be empowered and inspired to strong, collective action. But how?

Chomsky has a few suggestions, as we have seen. He also writes:

> Throughout the world, indigenous societies are struggling to protect what they sometimes call 'the rights of nature,' while the civilized and sophisticated scoff at this silliness. (Chomsky 2015a: 146)

So we should follow the lead of the developing countries and first-world nations and stop scoffing at them (and stop scoffing the earth's resources, if I can be allowed a small play on words). It's clear that we need to leave fossil fuels in the ground.

Perhaps we need to remind Alex that increasing freedom, justice, and democracy, removing the threat of nuclear annihilation, and tackling the climate crisis are all parts of the same task—see the next chapter for more on this. Despite the corporate propaganda, most Americans are on board. In other countries, even more of the population agrees. If I can sound off for a moment: we need to remember that humans may disagree about many issues, and we may fight and hate each other some of the time. But on the big issues, we are united. Take a look at this picture:

This man and I perhaps disagree about many things. But I want his child to survive and flourish, and I would like to think that the feeling is mutual.

Carl Sagan, the great American scientist, once said that the technology that carries nuclear weapons can also take us to the stars. We have the potential in our hands to destroy our planet, or to build a world without the threat of environmental apocalypse. May I suggest that we choose the latter?

Chomsky writes:

> What are the prospects for survival then? They are not bright. But the achievements of those who have struggled for centuries for greater freedom and justice leave a legacy

that can be taken up and carried forward–and must be, and soon if hopes for decent survival are to be sustained. (Chomsky 2014b)

10. Democracy in America

> It comes as no big surprise that "politics is the shadow cast
> on society by big business"—I'm quoting America's leading
> twentieth-century social philosopher John Dewey, who added
> quite realistically that "attenuation of the shadow will not
> change the substance." (Chomsky 2014a: 45)

L et's start by reviewing the key points from previous
chapters about Chomsky's politics.

Education

Most current education is designed to make people ignorant,
competitive, and conformist. The most educated people are
typically the most indoctrinated and tend to adopt current
orthodoxy unthinkingly. They would dispute this fiercely because
they have no memory of being forced to believe anything; and also
because everyone likes to think of themselves as independent and
critical. But in order to make it through the education system and
into well-paid jobs, you need to adopt the mindset of well-trained
lackeys which, as stated above, can be summed up as ignorant,
competitive, and conformist.

Anarchism

This is mostly a critical attitude towards structures of power and
authority: these systems always need to justify themselves, and if
they can't, they should be demolished. It also means extending

democracy to all the important areas of life, including investment, work, housing, healthcare, the wider economy, foreign policy, and the natural environment.

Propaganda

Businesses that own newspapers and commercial broadcasting are profit-making corporations. In the US, most media outlets are owned by big companies. The commercial media sell their product (that is, their audience) to other large corporations, who pay to advertise in them. Given this state of affairs, we should expect that the media promote the interests of their owners. Herman and Chomsky call this "The Propaganda Model," but they say that it is just a banal truism, and is amply confirmed by the way the media operate. As most United States citizens—unlike those in many other countries—do not live in fear of state terror, huge efforts are made by elites to control their minds instead.

Korea and the Middle East

US foreign policy is designed by the rich and powerful (another truism). Its primary aim is to shape the world so that American corporations can make profits everywhere, either by extracting raw materials or by selling US products, including vast amounts of expensive weapons. The main allies of the US are powerful elites in each country who help to implement this policy. The main enemies are popular local movements, which oppose this policy and are supported by much of the population. In South Korea, the main US allies have been wealthy and influential people who control the nation's economy; the main enemies have been the nationalist organizations in the North, which continue to run their part of the country. In the Middle East, the main allies have been elites in Saudi Arabia and similar brutal regimes, with Israel as the local police force, heavily armed and willing to crush nationalist movements.

The nuclear threat

Nuclear weapons are very profitable and very dangerous: only good luck has prevented them from killing hundreds of millions of people since the US used them in 1945. They need to be eliminated: it would help a lot if the major nuclear states fulfilled the obligations they committed to in various treaties, and moved towards nuclear disarmament.

Climate crisis

It is bad and getting worse, as most people realize. We can change our behavior as individuals, but the important solutions are global and political: we need governments at every level to take the actions that many of them talk about (except in the current US government)—notably, to keep fossil fuels in the ground, change food production and distribution, develop renewable energy sources, and care about millions of human beings in poor countries who are already the ones who suffer most.

The underlying problem

Why is all this happening? [Truism alert!] As we saw above in the words of John Dewey, as long as big business corporations have so much power, governments will only follow the will of voters if the corporations approve. That's the basic reason popular policies rarely get implemented. Chomsky notes, for example, that health care reform in the US foundered under President Obama for this very reason. An overwhelming majority wanted to free healthcare from the grip of giant health insurance companies. Obama said that this was "politically impossible," meaning that these corporations were opposed to it. The US media, of course, followed this line slavishly. The result: the Affordable Care Act (Obamacare), was a good first step, but never became the program that most Americans wanted. That's just one example.

If the popular vote makes little difference, and powerful business elites make the important decisions, what is the most likely result? A moment's thought suggests that:

- Candidates for election would not talk about their policies, since these policies are designed to harm ordinary people.
- They would concentrate on "cultural issues," usually a euphemism for stoking fear of black people, feminists, immigrants, the LGBTQ community, and so on.
- Media reports of election campaigns would highlight trivial things like candidates' speaking manner, or endorsement by celebrities, or the size of Donald Trump's hands, or pictures of candidates in cowboy costume on horseback (a routine trope for US Republicans).
- Insignificant differences between candidates would be blown up into huge fights, giving the misleading impression that the contenders for political offices are miles apart on the big issues.
- Political parties would become machines for raising money and promoting candidates at election time, rather than permanent places of political education and debate.
- Vote-rigging, and tampering with constituency boundaries would be rampant.[1] Measures to make it hard for poor people to vote would be pervasive.
- Many people would not bother to vote, feeling (correctly) that

it's a waste of time.

This sounds depressingly familiar to me, especially if we look at US elections and realize that fewer voters bother to vote in national elections than in any other large democracy. Take away the cowboy costumes, and you have an increasingly accurate snapshot of British politics too.[2]

So what is to be done? Well, in a democracy, governments are elected and are supposed to put into practice the will of voters. Despite the incessant propaganda in the media, most voters in the US are far to the left of both main political parties—according to opinion polls on specific issues, often cited by Chomsky.

For example, he notes that "polls consistently reveal that the public favors cutbacks in military rather than social programs, and even favor increased taxes if these are necessary for the programs of social welfare, environmental protection, work safety standards, women's rights, urban aid, etc." (1989b: 119)

This is also true in the UK, where huge majorities want to stop privatization of the National Health Service, rebuild the Children's Services that are in crisis because of underfunding, re-nationalize the railways, and build a welfare system which doesn't punish and humiliate disabled people.

What does Chomsky advise us to do about this? You may remember his summary of anarchism in Chapter 4, which I'll repeat here because I like it:

Any structure of power and authority needs to be challenged to justify itself. If—as is usually the case—it cannot be justified, it should be dismantled.

Anything more specific?

Well again, if you've been paying attention, you will know that Chomsky rarely gives specific tactical advice. Look around you, see what needs to be done, find allies, and start dismantling. You don't need to ask Chomsky for permission. But do read him from time to time—it will help to keep your head clear. (See also chapter 17.)

11. What is Language? The "Basic Property"

> The most basic property of language [is this]: each language provides an unbounded array of hierarchically structured expressions that receive interpretations at two interfaces, sensorimotor for externalization and conceptual-intentional for mental processes. (Chomsky 2016: 4)

Politics is important and hard work, but it isn't actually very complicated. Linguistics is different, and Chomsky's linguistics is not easy. I will try to keep it understandable, but you will have to work harder than in the previous chapters. In fact, you are probably lost already after the quote above. Don't worry: Chomsky's starting point for thinking about language is hard to grasp. You may think it is complex and strange, defying common sense, and you'd be right. This chapter tries to explain what Chomsky means by "the most basic property of language."

It gets worse. Chomsky continues:

> At the very least, then, each language incorporates a computational procedure satisfying the Basic Property. Therefore a theory of the language is by definition a generative grammar, and each language is what is called in technical terms an I-language—"I" standing for internal, individual, and intensional.

And then he says:

> I-language [is] a biological property of humans, some subcomponent of (mostly) the brain, an organ of the mind/ brain in the loose sense in which the term "organ" is used

in biology. I take the mind here to be the brain viewed at a certain level of abstraction. The approach is sometimes called the biolinguistic framework. It is regarded as controversial but without grounds, in my opinion.

Everything in the next few chapters depends on understanding these three quotes. In this part of the book, I will try to explain why Chomsky sees language in this way and the consequences of his way of thinking.

Here are some headlines:

Biology

The fact that I speak and understand English is a biological fact about me. Part of my brain has English stored in it. If I spoke Punjabi, that part of my brain would store Punjabi. That's a truism (cf. chapter 2).

Computation

We can analyze something as a computational procedure if it takes a symbol as input and transforms it into a different symbol following purely formal (mechanical, algorithmic) rules. Addition and other operations in arithmetic are computational procedures. What Chomsky calls the "Basic Property" of every human language can be modeled in this way, as we shall see. This has nothing to do with computers: *computational* means "involving computation," not "involving a computer." Chomsky does not think a comparison with computers is helpful in understanding human language.

Brain science

Now for some details, starting with biology. Chomsky sees human language as part of human biology. He says that this is in fact how most people see language because the only coherent notion of a language—English, Punjabi, or whatever—is a mental one. To say that two people speak Punjabi is to say that each of them has a part of their mind where their knowledge of Punjabi grammar, vocabulary, pronunciation, and so on is stored. This knowledge may not be conscious, but its existence cannot reasonably be doubted. It is evident from the behavior of Punjabi speakers when they use the language. So each language is ultimately *individual* and *internal*, as Chomsky says in the second quote above (don't worry about *intensional* for now: we'll return to that in Chapter 14). **Punjabi is a mental system, and when we study Punjabi grammar, we are studying part of the minds of Punjabi speakers.**

Saying that Punjabi is something "mental" or part of someone's mind, may sound mysterious and unscientific. Chomsky disagrees strongly. Language involves physical parts of our biological make-up: we need ears to hear speech, vocal cords, a tongue, and other "speech organs" in the upper body and head to produce speech, and eyes to read. Without links to the brain, though, our ears, speech organs, and eyes wouldn't work for language, or much else. (Our tongue has other functions, to do with tasting and swallowing food, but these also wouldn't work without our brain controlling them). Without a brain equipped to understand language, we wouldn't have language in any useful sense. Brain science, also called cognitive science or cognitive psychology, is the branch of biology that studies the human brain. **Chomsky sees linguistics as a branch of brain science.**

Sometimes it is possible to study the brain directly, either by (a) dissecting the brains of dead people, or (b) noting what happens when people lose part of their brain by accident, birth defect or surgery, or (c) using (hopefully harmless) scanning techniques such as Magnetic Resonance Imaging (MRI). Much of brain science, however, uses indirect methods that involve observing how people behave in particular circumstances. Doctors diagnose mental health problems in this way: autism, depression, and eating disorders have distinct patterns of behavior that experts can recognize and (in some cases) treat. **Language mostly has to be studied in this indirect way, but for Chomsky, it is still ultimately part of brain science**.

We normally talk about *mental* health, not *brain* health. Psychologists study the *mind*, while biologists study the *brain*. Psychologists know that the terms they use to study the mind–*thought*, *emotion*, *memory*, etc.–must have physical counterparts in the brain, but often they are not concerned about the brain as a physical object. The words 'mind' and "mental" are convenient abstract terms for part of our biology, and the study of mental phenomena is legitimate and useful. **For Chomsky, linguistics studies the parts of our mind–ultimately, the brain–which constitute language.**

So far, everything that I've said would be described by Chomsky (rightly in my view) as banal and obvious truisms. For him, the only coherent notion of a language is a mental one–ultimately a biological one. He also says that this is tacitly or explicitly assumed by everyone who deals with language.

More on computation

Now we return to *computation*. The essential point is that sentences aren't just sequences of words: the words combine into structures, which in turn combine to form larger structures. Look at this short sentence (it isn't true, in fact–see below–but that doesn't matter for now).

Communication is the fundamental property of human language.

It consists (I would argue) of three parts:

Communication	is	the basic property of human language
1	2	3

I can't justify this analysis in detail here, but if you think either of the following alternative analyses is better, linguists would say that you are wrong:

Communication–is the fundamental–property of human language.

Communication is the–fundamental property of–human language.

In my analysis, the first word of the sentence is a unit that linguists call a *noun phrase*, consisting of the noun *communication*. The last six words of the sentence combine into another noun phrase: it contains the noun *property*, preceded by the definite article *the* and the adjective *fundamental*, and followed by a prepositional phrase *of human language*. The verb *is* connects these two noun phrases to form a sentence. Don't panic if you can't follow these details: the essential point is that we have here a simple example of a sentence with a hierarchical structure: smaller parts (words) combine into larger parts (phrases), and then these larger parts combine into even larger units (bigger phrases, and ultimately a sentence).

"Combining"

What is the simplest possible way to describe a structure consisting of smaller parts repeatedly combining into larger parts? The answer: suppose that the grammar of English contains an instruction that simply says "Combine x with y." Let's call this the *Combining* rule. In our example, this rule can take the words *fundamental* and *property*, and combine them into the larger unit *fundamental property*. Repeated application of *Combining* ultimately gives us an analysis of the whole sentence with its structure.

Obviously, *Combining* isn't the whole story about our example sentence. The grammar of English needs to provide some extra information; it needs to restrict what can combine with what: the adjective *fundamental* can combine with the noun *property*, but the adjective has to come first—unlike a language like French, where the noun would have to come first (*le trait fondamental*, not **le fondamental trait*). The verb *eat* couldn't be used instead, to form **eat property*, partly because *eat* is a verb and not an adjective, and partly because we don't tend to eat properties. All this extra information has to be in the grammar—the minds—of English speakers. Chomsky doesn't disagree. His suggestion is that this extra information has to be learned by infants, but *Combining* doesn't: it is part of Universal Grammar (UG), a biological property that all humans share. We'll explore UG in the next chapter.

Merge

Chomsky's name for *Combining* is *Merge*, which I'll use from now on. *Merge* looks like this: take any two items X and Y and combine them into a new structure Z. If *Merge* is not restricted at all, then Z will be the set {X,Y}: in this set, X and Y are otherwise unchanged, and they can appear in any order.

What Chomsky calls *Merge* is an example of a *computational procedure*. As mentioned above, it has nothing to do with computers. Chomsky does not think the mind is a computer, or that an analogy with computers is helpful in understanding human language. A huge amount of time and money has been spent trying to program computers so they can produce and understand language as humans do. Chomsky says that this work has not yielded much insight into the question "What is language?" Some of the results have been of practical use: *Google Translate*, though limited, is convenient when a poor translation is better than no translation. That's helpful engineering, not science.

If a computational procedure is not a computing procedure or a computer procedure, what is it? Technically speaking, as I stated above, it's a procedure that takes a symbol as input and transforms it into a different symbol following purely formal (mechanical, algorithmic) rules. Addition and many other operations in arithmetic are computational procedures. So is *Merge*, which is not part of arithmetic, though the notion "the set {X, Y}" uses the term *set* from set theory, a different branch of mathematics. There is a field of study that investigates computational procedures: the field is sometimes called *Formal Language Theory*, though "language" is used in a technical sense here and doesn't mean "human language." (See Révész 2015 for an introduction. Révész talks about computer programs, algorithms, mathematics, and logic, but not about human languages.)

Some computational procedures are *unbounded*, meaning that they can apply and re-apply without limit. Addition is one: in principle, we can go on adding numbers forever, and there is no largest number. We use the word "infinity," but that isn't a number—it's a name for the fact that there isn't such a number. (Similarly, there is no such number as the square root of minus 1, but mathematicians still give it a name, the letter *i*.) Language is like the numbers in this respect: there is no such thing as "the largest possible sentence of English" (or any language). In theory, you can always add "... but I don't agree" to any sentence, even an enormous one. Obviously, it is physically impossible for any person to produce a sentence containing a trillion words, but that's a fact about the human body, its physical limitations, and its life expectancy, not a fact about language. That's what Chomsky means when he uses the word "unbounded" in the quote we started with.

So from a computational point of view, human language is unbounded and hierarchically structured. Chomsky argues that we can capture both of these characteristics if we make *Merge* "recursive"–that is, able to apply to its own output. So the new structure Z, in our formulation of *Merge* above, can in turn combine with other structures, including X and Y. That is how *Merge* captures the basic property of human language because it provides "an unbounded array of hierarchically structured expressions" in the simplest possible way.

Minimalism

It is conceivable, of course, that *Merge* is too simple to account for the types of unbounded hierarchical structures that we find in human languages, so that *Merge* needs to be complicated in some way. The point here is that any such complication has to be justified with evidence. This is the thinking behind the *Minimalist Program*, a key feature of Chomsky's latest work. The Minimalist Program starts with the assumption that *Merge* can be kept simple in analyzing every aspect of every human language: when evidence is presented which seems to cast doubt on that assumption, researchers look to see whether the evidence is genuine, and if it is, whether the complications are necessary. The assumption is known as the Strong Minimalist Thesis (SMT). Note the difference between a "Program," which is just an agenda for research, and a "Thesis," which is a scientific hypothesis–about language, in this instance. Chomsky believes that the SMT is currently standing up well, and is worth pursuing, though he expresses normal scientific caution about its ultimate success.

Sounds and meanings

By now you may be asking "What about the sounds of language, and what about the meanings that we communicate using language?" These are reasonable questions, because they are the aspects of language that we notice most: when someone speaks to us, we listen to the sounds they make, and we try to understand the meaning of what they say. Chomsky doesn't ignore these aspects: in the first quote above, he speaks of how the basic structures of language combine with "two interfaces, sensorimotor for externalization and conceptual-intentional for mental processes." The first of these is the part of the brain that deals with sounds (or gestures in sign language), and the second one deals with meanings. We are generally aware of sounds and meanings, and take the basic property for granted, unless it is violated. If it is wildly violated, we notice that immediately. Compare these two sentences:

> (a) One day even the state of Mississippi, a state sweltering with the heat of injustice, sweltering with the heat of oppression, will be transformed into an oasis of freedom and justice.

> (b) Justice and freedom of oasis an into transformed be will, oppression of heat the with sweltering, injustice of heat the with sweltering state a, Mississippi of state the even day one.

Whether a person recognizes (a) as part of Martin Luther King's "I have a dream" speech depends on their individual experience, but no native speaker of the language will doubt that (a) is a well-formed sentence of English while (b) is not. This may seem obvious, but it isn't trivial. Speakers of English can only begin to understand the meaning of sentence (a) once they have analyzed its structure. They usually do that analysis effortlessly and without conscious thought, but that doesn't mean it is simple—far from it. Compare: we usually walk on two legs effortlessly and without conscious thought, but that is a fearsomely complex achievement once you investigate it scientifically, and most animals can't do it (see the next chapter for more about this). The things that humans do mechanically and with ease appear simple, but that's usually, Chomsky maintains, because they are part of our biology.

Modularity

A word about *externalization*: language is internal to our brains, and Chomsky claims that most of our use of language stays there, in thoughts and what he calls "a kind of internal dialogue." He argues that our brains are *modular*: organized into discrete parts, *modules*, which have different internal structures. Obviously, these different parts have to interact: for example, the visual system has to communicate with the part of our brain that controls muscle activity so we can see a cup of coffee using our eyes and pick it up with our hand. Similarly, when we speak, the language module has to interact with other mental modules that control our speech organs (the mouth, tongue, lungs, etc.). Again, these are truisms.

Communication is not the "purpose" of human language

It's easy to assume that the "purpose" or "function" of language is to enable people to communicate with each other. That sounds so obvious: isn't it a "truism?" Well, no. Serious science can't assume that parts of our biology have a single "purpose." Is "the" purpose of our tongue to enable us to taste and swallow food or to make different vowel sounds? Do our hands have a single purpose? What about our hair: is it there to protect us from the sun, or to keep us warm, or to attract sexual partners? These questions are not helpful when you ask them like that. In general, biological evolution isn't a process that aims towards purposes (in technical parlance, evolution is not *teleological*–see Chapter 15 for more). Even worse, "communication" is not a clear notion. Flowers "communicate" with bees by displaying bright colors in the part of the spectrum that bees can see. The clothes we wear "communicate" things about us. Dogs "communicate" by urinating and sniffing traces left by other dogs.

Language is often used for communication: that is a genuine, but vague, truism. No doubt, having language has been central to human history, making it possible for us to build cities, wage wars, create art, and (sometimes) collaborate for the common good. Chomsky is not stopping anyone from investigating these aspects of language. But a careful study of language–an attempt to answer the question in the title of this chapter, "What is language?" has to probe deeper.

Language is so bound up with so many aspects of our lives that we often just assume that it's all about sounds used to communicate meanings. But without the basic property–unbounded hierarchical structure–there is no human language. Chomsky was not the first person to notice the basic property, but he has explored its consequences more consistently than anyone. His first achievement, back in the 1950s, was to apply formal language theory to analyze the basic property (drawing on work by British mathematician Alan Turing, among others). His work continues to reflect puzzlement about the basic property. Why does human language have the basic property? What part does this property play when we use language to say things and to understand what other people say? How does the basic property contribute to the way young people acquire language? Every part of Chomsky's work in linguistics has been driven by these questions.

12. Universal Grammar

Human language acquisition is instinctive, [...] based on a specialized "language organ"–one of many learning mechanisms within the brain [that] are neural circuits whose structure enables them to perform one particular kind of computation. (Chomsky 2002: 84)

T his chapter and the next one are mostly about how young people acquire a language. Notice that we say "acquire" a language, not "learn" a language–and "language acquisition" rather than "language learning." This is because the process is importantly different from how we usually learn something. Acquiring our first, native language doesn't involve teaching, textbooks, classes, exams, or any of the usual adjuncts to "learning." Nor does first language acquisition involve much conscious mental effort. It just "kind of happens:" as Chomsky puts it, language "grows" in young people.

Remember that I am talking about spoken language here–what every young person usually acquires, apart from people with a severe pathology. Reading and writing have to be learned–they do involve teaching, books, and so on, and often considerable mental effort.

"Universal Grammar" might sound mysterious, but it isn't. The term refers to the part of language that is genetic, and is therefore a component of every human language. If the Strong Minimalist Thesis (see previous chapter) is correct, then Universal Grammar is simply the Basic Property, and is captured by *Recursive Merge.*

Language, teething, and walking

I am going to compare first language acquisition, in some detail, with teething and walking. If that sounds strange, consider these facts:

Growing teeth, walking, and starting to talk, are part of the development process of every young person in the early years of life, pathology apart, as noted. They are among the main developmental milestones that parents or carers expect (along with eating solid food, using a toilet, and so on). Roughly speaking, teething usually begins in the first year of life, walking in the second year, and language starts in the second year as well, but really takes off in the third year.

Teething

Teething (the technical term is *dentition*) is a genetically determined maturational process that happens to the human body after birth. We aren't born with teeth, but we don't learn to grow them, and we can't normally do anything to make teeth appear–they just do, in their own time. The first set of "baby" teeth are normally replaced by "adult" teeth a few years later. All this is controlled by our genes. Teeth just grow–they are part of our biological development as humans. For another example of this kind of biological process, think of the physical changes during puberty.

Bipedalism

Walking on two legs (technically known as *bipedal gait*, or *bipedal locomotion*, or *bipedalism*) is a little more complicated. We are not born able to walk immediately (unlike the ability to breathe, or suck milk). This is different from newborn horses and cattle, for example, which usually try to stand upright and move about as soon as they are born. Babies do not have strong enough leg muscles to support their weight, and their center of gravity is so high, because of their large heads in relation to the rest of their bodies, that bipedal (two-legged) walking has to wait until their lower bodies catch up.

As babies reach the end of the first year of life, they can increasingly stand and support their weight, and then to move on two feet. As their center of gravity gets lower, they fall less often. Importantly, though, they have to develop the mental ability to balance and to control their limbs in a way that enables them to move forward. This is another genetically determined maturational process, but now it involves the mind as well as the relevant physical organs, unlike teething. Young people appear to be driven to walk by their genes. Encouragement and physical assistance can help, but the basic process is genetic and is part of what makes us human: no amount of encouragement or assistance will enable a newborn horse to walk easily and effortlessly on two legs.

What about language?

Like teething and walking, we can't use language at birth. Like walking, it involves the development of the mind as well as the relevant organs of the body (the lungs, tongue, ears, and so on). Chimpanzees have lungs, tongues, and ears similar to ours, but they don't have the mental ability to manipulate their breathing to make speech sounds; and however good their hearing is, they do not have the mental ability to distinguish speech sounds from the other noises that surround them. Apart from severe pathology, as noted above, language develops at roughly the same time in all young people, which strongly suggests that this mental and physical process is partly controlled by our genes.

This mental ability is a crucial similarity between walking and language. It is mostly unconscious: normally we don't consciously decide how we walk, we just do it, and the same is true of language. We can consciously change how we walk, of course, and we can deliberately talk differently too. But the basic abilities are stored in our brain and we just take them for granted. Insects like ants that have six legs walk in a different way–this ability is also stored in their brains and is mostly, or perhaps entirely, genetic. (Do young ants struggle to learn how to walk? If so, the process is partly learned. If not, it is at least in part genetic. I know little more about young ants, except that I prefer them to keep away from my kitchen. For some interesting work which aims to distinguish innate and learned behavior in young ants of one species, see Cammaerts 2014.)

A computational approach to walking

Scientists have a fairly solid understanding of what must be stored in our brains to enable us to walk. Please stay with me as I spell out some of it. Walking is, in essence, moving forward without falling over. It involves a series of movements, repeated in what is called the *gait cycle*. A good place to start the description of the cycle is the point at which we lean forward slightly. We then prevent ourselves from falling over by moving one of our feet forward. This moves the body's center of gravity (CoG) forward beyond the front of that foot, so–again, to prevent a fall–we move the other foot forward. We adjust our muscles, mostly of the legs and feet, so we can move our legs forward and at the same time support our body weight on one leg while the other one is moving forward.[1]

The details of how we do this are complex. The human foot and ankle, for example, contain 20 separate muscles. In order to organize the gait cycle while using the minimum amount of energy, our brain and central nervous system need to co-ordinate these muscles and many others. Our brain also has to harness the energy created when we nearly fall over, so that each near-fall contributes to our forward motion. Falling creates what is called *potential energy*, and the amount of this energy depends on gravity, how heavy we are, and the height of our CoG. To harness this energy, it has to be converted into *kinetic energy*, the kind created by the muscles, causing us to move forward: the amount of this energy depends on our body weight and the speed with which our CoG is moving forward. So mathematically, we have:

Potential energy in joules = mgh, where m is the mass of the body, g is acceleration due to gravity, and h is the height of the CoG of the body.

Kinetic energy in joules = 0.5 mv2, where = m is the mass of the body, and v is the velocity of the CoG of the body.

The most efficient way to convert the potential energy from falling into kinetic energy for moving forward is to do it at the places in the gait cycle where the potential energy is at its maximum. There are two such places: when only one foot is on the ground, pushing the body upwards, and the CoG is therefore at its highest point. These are also the places where the kinetic energy is lowest, in need of help. In this way, the gait cycle enables an efficient transfer of energy from falling to moving forward. (This also means that we move forward quite smoothly, rather than in a series of bone-jarring jerks).

When we walk, our brains perform—unconsciously—these calculations (and many others) to make bipedal locomotion happen. The calculations express our best understanding of part of the essential nature of walking. They form part of an abstract, mathematical model of walking. Any scientific analysis of walking has to include this model. You don't have to be interested in this science: you may care more about how to keep fit by walking, or where to walk for fun. But for scientists, doctors, physiotherapists, and sports coaches the science of walking is fundamental, and these calculations are part of the foundations of that science. Exactly how our brains do these calculations is far from understood: neuroscientists have started to isolate the parts of the brain that are involved, but there is still much work to be done.

This account of walking parallels Chomsky's view of language. The basic property of language–unbounded hierarchical structure–has to be part of our mental make-up in a similar way to the physics of walking. Learning to walk involves (among other things) unconsciously mastering this physics. Acquiring language involves (among other things) unconsciously applying the computation of the basic property to the sounds we hear around us. Both processes are in part genetically determined, and they are essentially the same in every human (again, pathology aside).

Some crucial differences

Now we get to some differences between language and the other two human abilities. If we weigh up nature (our genes) versus nurture (the environment), teething is a purely physical process which seems to be entirely driven by nature. Walking is also almost completely genetic, differing from teething in that it has mental as well as physical aspects. Language is like walking in this respect, but it is different in that we all walk in basically the same way, with minor style differences. Which language we pick up as infants depends entirely on our environment, though, and there are several thousand very different and often mutually incomprehensible human languages.

So walking is basically invariant across the human species, whereas there are thousands of different languages. Young people don't acquire "language" in general–they acquire *a* language, normally the one they hear around them. If they are surrounded by people speaking Punjabi, they will acquire Punjabi. If they have never been exposed to English, they will not acquire English. When we hear a language being spoken which we have not mastered, it isn't just that we don't understand it–usually, we can't even segment the stream of sounds into words. We may be aware that we are hearing speech: we may infer that the person is speaking some language or other from the context, the tone of voice, the facial expressions and the hand gestures, the give and take of a conversation, the occasional recognizable word, and so on. But languages differ hugely from each other, whereas there are no such differences in the realm of bipedalism.

This means that acquiring a language isn't purely genetic, as teething, puberty, and walking are. Acquiring a language requires input from the people who interact with human infants. The words and grammar that children acquire are those of the language that they hear around them. The linguistic sounds that they distinguish and produce are likewise those of their immediate environment. This is probably one reason Chomsky's insistence on the genetic component of language acquisition has met a lot of resistance. Punjabi and English are not 'innate', not part of our genetic endowment. Which part of language, then, is genetic?

Chomsky's answer is: the basic property is genetic, while "externalization" can take many different forms, depending on the environment. The basic property sets limits on the type of language that can be acquired by children, but within those limits, the sounds, and the structure and meanings of words can vary depending on each child's experience.

Structure-dependence

Let's look at how the basic property—unbounded hierarchical structure—sets limits. Chomsky makes a crucial distinction between *string-dependent* and *structure-dependent* procedures. Sentences are more than just strings of words: as we have seen, a sentence consists of words which combine to form phrases, which in turn combine to form larger phrases, which combine to form sentences: this idea of units repeatedly combining is, Chomsky hopes, modeled by the procedure that he calls *merge*. Sentences have a structure.

Here's a simple example: start with a statement:

I can have a drink

How could we turn this into a question? Speakers of English know that we do it by moving the word *can* to the front:

Can I have a drink?

We can use a string-dependent procedure to capture this knowledge: *Move the second word to the front.* Putting it that way means treating the statement as a string–a sequence–of words. But English speakers know that this procedure doesn't work for slightly more complex statements like this one:

My sister can have a drink.

If we moved the second word to the front, we would get the wrong result:

*Sister my can have a drink?

(The asterisk just indicates that this is not a possible English sentence). Instead, the form of the question should be:

Can my sister have a drink?

A procedure that covers this example and the simple one is: *Move the auxiliary verb to the left of the subject noun phrase.* That's a structure-dependent procedure: it involves the notions *noun phrase* and *subject*, which refer to units larger than words; and the notion *auxiliary verb*, which refers to the relation between *can* and *have*–again, more than just where *can* appears in the sequence of words.

When young people acquire their first language they don't use string-dependent procedures to figure out the patterns in the stream of sounds–"acoustic disturbances," as they are sometimes called–that they hear around them. They don't use string-dependent procedures to make new sentences; they use structure-dependent ones. Chomsky argues that we must be innately (i.e., genetically) programmed to use structure-dependent procedures: otherwise, you would expect some children to try the simpler procedure. This doesn't seem to ever happen.

Not just repetition

But, you may be thinking, children never hear an adult say *Sister my can have a drink?* So you wouldn't expect them to say it either. Perhaps surprisingly, this is not how language acquisition works. Children often say things that they have never heard. To take a simple example, many of the most common verbs in English have irregular past tense forms: instead of just putting a -d on the end, which is the pattern for regular verbs like *laugh, live,* and *love,* we say *was, had, came, brought, spoke* and *sang.* But my children, like most children, went through a phase when they said *comed, bringed* and *speaked* when they were little—words that they had never heard but which "regularized" these verbs, so that they behaved like *laughed* and *lived.* This tendency to over-extend a rule for a while rather than learn exceptions is quite normal in language acquisition. Children don't just imitate—they look for general procedures. Maybe that in itself isn't germane only to language: perhaps children learn lots of things in this way, consciously or (as with language) unconsciously. It's the fact that they only look for structure-dependent general procedures which is the most important evidence that the basic property of language is innate.

Here's another example to illustrate the difference between string-dependence and structure-dependence. Look at this sentence:

People who laugh often live longer.

This has two possible meanings:

(a) People who frequently laugh, live longer

(b) People who laugh, live longer a lot of the time.

The adverb *often* in our sentence can either go with *laugh* to its left to give (a) or with *live* to its right to give (b). Now suppose we put *often* at the front:

Often, people who laugh live longer.

In this version, there is no ambiguity: *often* has to go with *live*, as in (b) above. We simply can't use this version to mean (a).

Why not? Here we have to think computationally again. When we start a sentence with *often*, we need to find another word, usually a verb, for it to modify. The simplest candidate would be the nearest verb, the first one. But that strategy doesn't work here: instead of the first verb, the strategy that we actually employ is to look for the verb that is structurally closest. Although *laugh* comes first, it is inside a relative clause (*who laugh*). The verb *live*, on the other hand, is the main verb, the one that is structurally closest to the subject *people*, even though it is not closest to *people* in the linear order of the words in the sentence. The strategy that we in fact use is not the simple one, "look for the first verb" but the more complex one, "look for the verb that is structurally closest." The idea of "structural closeness" might be hard to grasp, but you don't need to understand all the details. The key idea is that we (always) use the structure of the sentence to help us understand it, not just the order of the words (first, second, etc.).

Chomsky argues that this is *always* the type of strategy that we use. We don't use *string-dependent* computational procedures, which just deal with the order of words in a sentence. We use *structure-dependent* procedures, which involve the structural organization of sentences. Every language works like this, and there is no obvious reason: it doesn't seem to make communication easier, structure-dependent procedures are more complex (from a computational point of view) than string-dependent ones, and animal communication systems do not work like this. The only possible explanation is a genetic one: the part of our brain that does language has the basic property built into it.

Chomsky has for a long time used the term *Universal Grammar* (UG) for the genetic part of language. The term emphasizes that UG is part of every human language. As we saw in the last chapter, the simplest hypothesis is that UG simply is the Basic Property, and that recursive *Merge* captures this property. So Chomsky currently speculates (his word) that UG (a.k.a. the Language Organ) equals *Merge*.

13. Language Acquisition

[Child language acquisition is] a process better described as "growth" than "learning," in my opinion. Chomsky (2000: 120)

S o far, I haven't said anything specific about how children acquire language. Is there empirical evidence that young people use *Merge* as part of this process? Before we look at some examples, remember that UG is supposed to explain what all languages have in common. We need some other mechanism to account for the *differences* between languages.

Questions about questions

Let's stick with questions, which vary in interesting ways from language to language. Here are some examples:

Language	Statement	Question	Procedure
English	You speak English.	Do you speak English?	Move the auxiliary verb to the front. If there isn't one, use the appropriate form of auxiliary *do*.
French	Tu parles Anglais.	Parles-tu Anglais?	Move the verb to the front. (In everyday spoken French it would probably be more normal to say something like "Tu parles anglais, toi?" It would be interesting, but take us too far afield to explore this. The version in the example is perfectly grammatical but more formal).
Spanish	Hablas Inglés.	¿Hablas Inglés?	Use question intonation, i.e., raise the pitch of your voice as you pronounce the sentence. (In writing, use an upside-down question mark at the start of the question, and a normal question mark at the end).
Latin	Loqueris Anglice.	Loquerisne Anglice?	Attach the question suffix *-ne* to the verb.

Every row in this table involves structure dependence (cf. the previous chapter), except for the intonation fact about Spanish (more on this below). Notions like "auxiliary" and "subject" are only available to speakers who have (unconsciously) analyzed a sentence into parts and smaller parts. So any analysis of questions in English, French, and Latin has to involve the *Merge* rule. No one thinks that *Merge* is the whole analysis: English speakers have to know that *speak* is not an auxiliary verb, French speakers need to be aware that *parles* is a verb, and Latin speakers must know that *loqueris* is a verb. This information is specific to each language and has to be learned from experience. But *Merge* has to be part of the analysis. How large a part is an open question—see the remarks about the Strong Minimalist Thesis in Chapter 10.

Spanish does not use *Merge*, or any grammatical device, to form questions, relying on intonation instead. This strategy is available in the other three languages too (*You speak English?*, with rising intonation, can be a question), but in Spanish, it is the only strategy.

Latin is one of many languages that has a special word (or a suffix in this case) to signal questions.

Clearly, there is a sense in which all four questions are "the same," even though the way they are formed is different in each language. One way to capture this is to show the meaning of the four questions like this:

Q YOU SPEAK ENGLISH

Here "Q" just means "question," and the expressions in upper case are supposed to be (language-independent) meanings, not English words. Then Q sets off or "triggers" the question procedure for that language, producing the sentences in the "Question" column in the table.

How do young children trying to master their native language work out how to ask and understand questions in that language? Presumably, they have to use information about the context: when they hear questions, which are quite common in everyday speech, they recognize that questions are special ways of obtaining information. They recognize too that asking questions is a useful skill for them to acquire. After that, UG takes over and does the rest (except in Spanish, as we saw), and they gradually acquire the Question Procedure for their language. So the full story about the acquisition of questions involves children analyzing the language spoken around them and picking one of the resources that UG makes available, moving items around as in English and French, adding special suffixes for Latin or some other mechanism in Spanish.

Pro-drop

You may have noticed another difference in the examples: English and French sentences need a subject pronoun (you, tu), whereas Spanish and Latin do not: the idea of "you" is expressed in these two languages as an ending on the verb. English doesn't have any ending on the verb *speak*, though (written) French does: the –s on *parles* is the second person singular ending, and works just like the Spanish –s and Latin –is endings–except that in French you can't just start a question with *Parles* on its own, without *tu*, unlike Spanish where *Hablas* doesn't need help from a pronoun.

This difference between languages like English and French on the one hand, and those like Spanish and Latin on the other, is known as the *Pro-drop Parameter*. A parameter is something that can vary (like height and weight), and "Pro drop" can be understood as "dropping the pronoun or not." This term assumes that Spanish and Latin start with a pronoun and "drop" it; another analysis might take the opposite viewpoint: we could assume instead that none of the languages has a pronoun to start with, and that English and French "add" them, while Spanish and Latin "drop" them.

What this illustrates is that working with UG raises new questions and research possibilities. People studying child language without being interested in UG (or actively rejecting the whole idea of UG) have long noted that some languages need subject pronouns, but other languages do not. They say, correctly, that these differences are easy for a child to spot: sentences expressing the ideas of "me" and "you" are widespread both in language directed to children, and in the language that children hear around them from adults and older children. So how children learn that their language is Pro-Drop or not is hardly a mystery.

For researchers interested in UG, that's just the beginning. As we saw, they go on to ask whether UG starts with pronouns and drops them in some languages, or starts without pronouns and adds them in other languages. They have also looked at a huge range of languages and discovered that some of them cannot be neatly slotted under one type or the other, so that the Pro-drop Parameter needs to be refined. They have also drawn on research into adult grammars within Chomsky's framework, which has linked this parameter with other ways that languages differ. Here are two examples:

- In pro-drop languages, the subject can appear after the verb in statements (as opposed to questions):

  Spanish: Hablas tu Inglés.

  English: *Speak you English.

- In pro-drop languages, you have to include the complementizer (the word corresponding to *that*) in certain kinds of questions.

  Spanish: ?Quien dijiste que habla Inglés? (Compare: *?*Quien dijiste habla Inglés?*)

  English: *Who did you say that speaks English? (Compare: *Who did you say speaks English?*)

Once the parameter has been "fixed" one way or the other, on the basis of evidence that is easy to spot, this should mean that children will not need much (or any) evidence to apply it in other areas of grammar. So once a child has worked out whether or not their language is pro-drop, the facts about the other two differences don't need to be learned–they follow immediately. Whether this is correct has been researched intensively, and I can't review that here–but the new questions have thrown up other questions and new methods for investigating them.

Some aspects of second language learning

It isn't news that learning a second language after early childhood is harder than, and looks different from, the almost effortless way that children acquire their native language. (I should add here that a large proportion of the world's children have two or more native languages, and manage to acquire them with little more effort than monolingual children). Does Chomsky's work shed any light on this, and does his framework have practical implications for how to teach second languages in schools and to adult learners?

Yes and yes. Once parameters have been set for a person's first language (L1), they may have to be set a different way for a second language (L2). English speakers learning Spanish have to learn to leave out the subject pronoun, and Spanish learners of English have to learn to put it in. Obviously, learning an L2 involves learning a lot of new words too. But one popular theory claims that the important grammatical differences between languages are not located in the general vocabulary (words like *speak/parler/hablar/loquor*) but in the "functional" expressions: endings on verbs and nouns, question words, and so forth, known as "functional morphology."

To see how this works, let's look again at questions in English and French. We saw that *Parles-tu anglais?* is OK in French, whereas *Speak you English?* is not possible in (modern) English. There is another difference between the two languages, which is apparently unrelated. Compare the position of the adverb *often/souvent* in these examples:

I often speak English.	*Je souvent parle Anglais
*I speak often English.	Je parle souvent Anglais

In English, the adverb *often* has to come before the verb, but in French, the equivalent adverb *souvent* has to come after the verb. No one ever pointed that out to me when I learned French at school—I just kind of picked it up. Recent work in second language acquisition suggests that once learners are taught about the difference between questions in French and English, the position of adverbs comes "for free." For some more on this, see Slabakova (2013): she also proposes that practicing functional morphology in "meaningful, plausible sentences" is a good strategy for learners—not abstract, artificial exercises, but with examples where the meaning and structure of the sentences is clear.

14. Meaning

For Chomsky, meaning is peripheral to linguistic form, a notion so preposterous it is hard to square it with the 20th century's most famous linguist. (Lukin 2011)

I t is sometimes said that Chomsky has no interest in semantics, the study of meaning. Indeed, he has occasionally given that impression:

> Natural language has no referential semantics in the sense of relations between symbols and mind-independent entities. Rather, it has syntax (internal symbol manipulation) and pragmatics (modes of use of language). Formal semantics, including model-theoretic semantics, falls under syntax in this categorization. (Chomsky 2016: 48)

Read this carefully to understand what Chomsky is saying here. "Mind-independent entities" are just things out there: tables, books, coffee, chinchillas, and so forth. The claim is that language is not linked to these things directly. Humans can use language to refer to these things, but the words and sentences of language do not themselves refer to these things.

Intensions

This takes us back to the term I-*Language* from Chapter 11, where "I" stands for "internal, individual, and intensional." The *intension* of a word is what we usually call its meaning: what you need to know about a word in order to use it correctly. More technically, this is the set of properties[1] that the word expresses. For the physical sense of the word *table*, these properties are (roughly):

- a piece of furniture
- with a flat top
- and one or more legs,
- providing a level surface for eating, writing, or working at

To use the word *table* correctly, this is the minimum that you need to know–alternatively, these are the properties that the word expresses. Some people know a lot more about tables: for example, they can distinguish coffee tables, dining tables, and bedside tables (see Home Stratosphere 2019 for a list of 43 types). Some people know how to transport tables safely in vans, or how much different tables cost. We can distinguish knowledge of the word *table* from knowledge about the things we call tables. The idea is that any speaker of English is likely to have the first type of knowledge, but only some have the second. It is not always easy, though, to draw the line between these two kinds of knowledge. See Riemer (2010: 100-2) for discussion.

It is sometimes assumed that that the word *table* refers to the objects in the world which have these properties. That is the assumption that Chomsky wants to reject. Clearly, humans can use the word to refer to such objects, but that is about our use of language–part of pragmatics. The word *table* does not refer to anything. In fact, words and sentences in general do not refer–people use them to describe the world (including imaginary worlds. My granddaughter talks about "unicorns" and "the earwax museum," which only exist in some people's imaginations).

This point might be easier to grasp if we move away from physical objects like tables. Words like *love*, *happiness*, *democracy*, and *forthrightness* have meanings–intensions–but it is a mistake to conclude that happiness is something out there in the world. That doesn't stop us from using the word when we talk to each other. For adjectives like *easy*, *obscene*, or *vibrant*, this is even more obvious, and when we get to the most common words–*the, a, and, of, yes,* and so forth–we use them all the time without imagining that they refer to anything. We can also talk about impossible things like "square circles" and "colorless green ideas" if we want.

Sounds and meanings

Chomsky likes to draw a parallel between the sounds of words and the meanings of words. As well as the meaning of *table*, speakers of English know that the word rhymes with *cable* and *stable*. Their brains contain instructions for making and combining the sounds in these words. Truism alert: their brains do not "contain" these sounds, whatever that might mean. The sounds exist out there, but it's only via our brains that we select them from the huge variety of sounds in the world and interpret them as speech sounds. Chimpanzees, chinchillas, and beetles are surrounded by the same sounds, but they can't interpret them as we do: our brains are wired by our genes to do it, but theirs are not. (Conversely, humans are surrounded by the same smells as dogs; but no matter how much we sniff each other from behind, we can't recognize most of those smells, and we can't use them to recognize each other. Our brains and noses are hard-wired differently from dog brains and noses.)

We can't, therefore, call phonology–the study of speech sounds–*intensional*, but we can call it *internal*, the first "I" in I-language. Many phonologists just assume that what they are studying is part of the human mind. Some linguists and philosophers believe semantics is different, but Chomsky sees no reason to think so. The bulk of phonology is about internal matters, to do with how our brains deal with the sounds of language. Phonologists need to know something about the study of sound in general–acoustics–and something about anatomy and physiology to investigate how our bodies hear and produce speech sounds. That's complex. The relation between language and how we use it in the real world is far, far more complex. In practice, semantics is generally internal.

If you regard language as a mental organ, part of human biology, then all this follows more or less automatically. Knowing a language—English, Punjabi, etc.—involves knowing the phonological (sound-related) and semantic (meaning-related) properties of the words of that language, and how to combine these words into sentences. Investigating this knowledge is a legitimate scientific activity. We can also examine how people use language (pragmatics), which may be interesting and practically useful, but is unlikely to be amenable to scientific inquiry, in Chomsky's view.

Some examples

The claim that Chomsky's linguistics ignores or marginalizes meaning is laughable. In Chapter 13, we looked at how four different languages formed questions, noting that the meaning of *Do you speak English?* / *Parles-tu anglais?* / *¿Hablas inglés?* / and *Loquerisne Anglice?* is the same in each language, and that any analysis has to capture this similarity along with the obvious differences.

In Chapter 12, we saw that the sentence:

People who laugh often live longer.

has two possible meanings: (a) People who frequently laugh, live longer, or (b) People who laugh, live longer a lot of the time. But if we put *often* at the front and say:

Often, people who laugh live longer.

there is no ambiguity: *often* has to go with *live*, as in (b) above. That was about *meaning* and *ambiguity*, central notions in semantics. Chomsky's linguistics is full of such discussions. One frequently used example is the contrast between the sentences *John is easy to please* and *John is eager to please*: with *easy*, John is on the receiving end of the pleasing, whereas with *eager*, it is John who is doing the pleasing. That's a semantic difference.

Word meaning

Much of what Chomsky says about meaning applies to sentences, but he also has strong views about the meaning of individual words. His point is that even apparently simple words are used in complex ways. A clear example is the word *book*, which can be used to talk about a physical object, or its contents, even before it exists. We can say

> That book is going to weigh two kilos, if Kim ever finishes writing it.

Here's a more complex example:

> A city is both concrete and abstract, both animate and inanimate: Los Angeles may be pondering its fate grimly, fearing destruction by another earthquake or administrative decision. London is not a place. Rather, it is at a place, though it is not the things at that place, which could be radically changed or moved, leaving London intact. London could be destroyed and rebuilt, perhaps after millennia, still being London [...] If London is reduced to dust, it—that is, London—can be re-built elsewhere and be the same city, London. If my house is reduced to dust, it (my house) can be rebuilt elsewhere, but it won't be the same house. If the motor of my car is reduced to dust, it cannot be rebuilt, though if only partially damaged, it can be. (Chomsky 1995: 21)

Chomsky argues that we cope quite easily with these different perspectives on the meaning of a word, suggesting that they are largely innate (just as *Merge* is innate).

These brief examples only give a small taste of the richness of Chomsky's work in semantics. I hope that they demolish the ignorant myth that Chomsky regards semantics as "peripheral."

15. Evolution

> We can suggest what seems to be the simplest speculation about the evolution of language. Within some small group from which we are all descended, a rewiring of the brain took place in some individual, call him Prometheus, yielding the operation of unbounded Merge. (Chomsky 2010a: 59)

O ur closest relatives, the great apes (*panins*), do not have language. Humans (*hominins*) do. Chomsky's explanation is a simple one: the great apes do not have *Merge* in their brains (cf. Chapter 11 on the "basic property"), whereas humans do. So the crucial part of the evolution of language reduces to the appearance of *Merge*. In what he calls "a fair guess," Chomsky proposes that an abrupt and small rewiring of the brain took place between 50,000 and 100,000 years ago in Africa, possibly in a single individual within a small group of hominins. This rewiring produced *Merge*. The abrupt change may have been a side effect of increased brain size, or it may have been a chance mutation.[1] All humans, Chomsky suggests, are descended from that small group. Language (considered as a mental organ) has not evolved since then: historical changes to particular languages over time do not involve modifications to *Merge*.

Chomsky argues that this small rewiring of the brain had huge consequences: in particular, it enriched the human capacities for complex thought and planning. This would have given the hominin with *Merge*, and his or her offspring, enormous advantages over other humans. Eventually, it would have led to early technology, artistic expression as seen in rock paintings, and the exodus from Africa to other parts of the world (Chomsky 2016: 25).

With this geographical spread of language-enabled humans, languages no doubt diversified. The fact that languages use different words for the same thing is easy to explain: groups of early migrating humans were separated by barriers such as mountains, rivers, and seas, and used different words for the same concept; they also encountered new animals and physical objects, for which they needed new names. It is less obvious why different sounds and grammars emerged. Chomsky says that the reason is simple: although *Merge* restricts the range of human languages (to structure-dependent ones, as we saw in Chapter 11), how language is externalized is less constrained. Hence phonological and grammatical variation–within the range limited by *Merge*–is not surprising.

In the rest of this chapter, I'll try to summarize some of the background information that will help you judge Chomsky's view of language evolution. I'll look at other recent work in the field, compare language with walking once more, say something about the timeline, and point out some common misconceptions about evolution.

The field of language evolution

There has been a huge amount of recent work on language evolution. A useful compendium, Tallerman & Gibson (2012), contains 65 chapters and runs to 790 pages. Chomsky is not impressed by most of this work, because it is based on what he calls "virtual dogma that has no serious support," namely that "the function of language is communication." Chomsky argues that if language has a basic function, it is to express thoughts, not communicate them. "Communication" is a vague notion: animals, and possibly also plants, "communicate" with each other, (Chomsky 2016: 15). See Chapter 11 for more about this.

An example of the kind of work that would leave Chomsky unimpressed is Dunbar (2012), summarizing a large range of the author's work. Dunbar argues that "language evolved to support a social function" and that "language does not exist in a vacuum, but rather requires a community of speakers who can use it. (2012: 343) More specifically, he claims that "primates use social grooming [cleaning each other's fur or skin–RS] to bond social groups," but that grooming takes time which often needs to be used to find and prepare food. The advantage of language, Dunbar says, is that it enables humans to bond while they are engaged in other activities, such as feeding or working. This supposedly enabled our hominin ancestors to form larger social groups.

Perhaps these claims are plausible–but they assume that communication in social groups is the most important function of language, and ask how this function evolved. They do not address the question of how the basic property of language–unbounded hierarchical structure–evolved. For Chomsky, this is the first and most fundamental question that needs to be addressed in work on language evolution.

This criticism of Dunbar is emphatically not that his claims are speculative. Given the shortage of evidence, theories of language evolution are bound to be speculative, including Chomsky's. The point is that Dunbar is speculating about the wrong things.

So the distinctive thing about human language, the thing that should be the central issue in an account of how language originally evolved, is the basic property, not communication. Chomsky often draws parallels with other areas of biology, such as insect vision. It would be absurd to study the evolution and growth of the eyes of bees and flies without first offering a coherent notion of what an "eye" is: this notion can be modified or refined in subsequent study, but the absence of such a notion would make no sense. The same is true in linguistics: first you need some notion of what language is, then you can go on to investigate how it develops in individuals and how it evolved in the species.

Another unhelpful assumption in much of the research, Chomsky claims, is that language equals speech: but speech is only one way to externalize language–sign language, and writing, are others–and furthermore, our ancestors were apparently able to make speech sounds for over a million years without having language.

For some criticisms of Chomsky's account of language evolution, see Tallerman 2014.

Language and walking ... again

Another thing that differentiates humans from most other animals is walking upright on two legs–*bipedal gait*, *bipedal locomotion*, or *bipedalism*, as scientists call it (Compare chapter 12 for more on walking). Most birds can walk on two legs (though some can only hop), but other mammals, particularly our closest relatives the primates, do not–or not exclusively. It is commonly assumed that our ancestors were not bipedal, and that they developed this ability after they had split off from the other hominids (notably the chimpanzees and bonobos) about seven million years ago (mya). It appears from the fossil evidence that bipedalism developed gradually from then on and that it was firmly established by three mya. There has been a lot of work on the evolution of bipedalism, much of it nicely summarized in Vaughan (2003). Vaughan considers the possibility that bipedalism is the most fundamental difference between humans and other primates: this is an interesting challenge to the view of Chomsky and many others that language is the most fundamental. I can't try to resolve that disagreement here.

It is not hard to imagine that the advantages of bipedalism–leaving the hands free, and being able to see farther, for example–gradually outweighed the disadvantages. The latter were far from trivial: changes in the shape of the human pelvis due to bipedalism, and increases in brain size at around the same time, meant that human babies had to be born earlier and therefore needed more parental care than baby chimpanzees and bonobos.

The big picture of language evolution seems to be different. Gradual increases in brain size, and anatomical changes to the jaw and throat, meant that the preconditions for spoken language probably evolved gradually. But though we had the precondition for thousands, possibly millions, of years, language as Chomsky understands it (the basic property captured by unbounded *Merge*) did not evolve until the abrupt change 50,000 to 100, 000 years ago. If that is correct, then the gradual evolution of bipedalism was very different from the rapid evolution of language.

Timeline of evolution

Language is a decidedly recent development compared with evolution as a whole. It has taken over three billion years for the original single-celled organisms to evolve into the species we see around us today. All known living things—plants, animals, bacteria, readers of this book—are descended from those original, single-celled organisms. Every single one contains the basic molecule of life, DNA. Common descent is the only serious explanation for that.

The earliest known fossils of terrestrial vertebrates date from about 350 mya. The first dinosaurs and mammals appeared around 250 mya. Around 16 mya, the common ancestor of humans (*hominins*) and chimpanzees and bonobos (*panins*) appeared, and the division between humans and chimps took place around six mya. The earliest humans probably lived mostly in trees, had protruding jaws and teeth as chimpanzees do, and small brains. Over several million years, humans developed bipedal walking, our jaws and teeth receded, and the size of our brains increased from about 350–400 cubic centimeters (cc) to around 1,350 cc.

The first modern (that is, anatomically similar to us) humans are thought to date from around two mya, and the earliest stone tools so far dated are from around that time too. So for most of modern human existence, we managed without language. The usual evidence of evolution—fossils, radiocarbon dating, population genetics, and embryology—tends to involve many millions of years, not tens of thousands, and doesn't help much with language evolution.

The big picture of evolution is controversial. I don't mean the attack from "creationists"–people who believe that the universe and various forms of life originated by divine intervention. Serious scientists agree that Darwin was basically right: all living things descended from a common single-celled ancestor over about three billion years through natural selection. The exact character of this process is a hot research topic, though: current work in genetics, neurology, embryology, and paleontology has provided new insights and raised new questions. From the 1930s onwards, most experts emphasized random mutation of genes; more recently, biologists have started to stress the development of seeds and embryos into plants and animals.

Misconceptions

To understand the processes of evolution, you have to get rid of some important misconceptions. One of these is the tendency to be human-centric: the idea that evolution necessarily leads to highly intelligent organisms like us. Well, the dinosaurs were not very intelligent, but they ruled the earth far longer than we have so far. If humans are still around 200 million years from now, then we can claim that we outlasted the dinosaurs, who held sway for about that length of time. The distinguished scientist J. B. S. Haldane is alleged to have said that if there is a God, he is "inordinately fond of beetles:" there are about 400,000 species of *coleoptera*, about a quarter of all known animal life-forms, and beetles have been around for at least 200 million years (cockroaches, which are not beetles, for even longer). Evolution does not have a purpose–it is just a part of nature.

Another misconception is that evolution is by definition a ruthless competition, as suggested by the phrase "survival of the fittest." What this expression actually means is that heritable traits that enable an organism to adapt to its local environment will tend to be those that are passed on to future generations. It may be that the first small group of hominins with language flourished because they were better able to collaborate, or plan ahead, or look after their offspring.[2,3]

A third misconception is that evolution is always a gradual process, involving a sequence of small changes, each of them beneficial in themselves. Chomsky argues against this picture: some humans have adapted recently to living at high altitudes, for example.

To sum up

Chomsky's account of language evolution is bold and distinctive, challenging much work in the field—rather like much of his linguistics, in fact. Some leading experts in evolution generally agree with him, notably Ian Tattersall. (see Tattersall 2017 for a good summary) Others are skeptical. As usual with Chomsky, you will have to decide for yourself.

16. Responsible and irresponsible intellectuals

It is the responsibility of intellectuals to speak the truth and to expose lies. Chomsky (1969a:257)

C homsky wrote an essay, first published in 1967, called "The responsibility of intellectuals" (references here are to the 1969 reprint). A conference was held in London in 2017 to celebrate the 50th anniversary of this essay, with Chomsky participating via a video link from Arizona. A book based on the conference came out in 2019 (Allott et al. 2019).

As well as speaking the truth, Chomsky's essay set out two other responsibilities of intellectuals: "to provide historical context; and to lift the veil of ideology, the underlying framework of ideas that limits the boundaries of debate." (Smith & Smith 2019: 6). In 1967, Chomsky was mostly concerned with the US invasion of Vietnam. He wrote scathingly about the distinction that was commonly drawn then between "responsible criticism" of US policy and "sentimental" or "emotional" or "hysterical" criticism by "wild men in the wings," in the words of McGeorge Bundy, an academic who was National Security Adviser to Presidents Kennedy and Johnson from 1961 to 1966. Chomsky gives many examples of what "responsible intellectuals" said: for example, David N. Rowe, a professor at Yale University, proposed to a Congressional Committee in 1966 that the US should buy all surplus Canadian and Australian wheat, so that there would be mass starvation in China (1969b: 267).

Chomsky was fierce in his condemnation of these mainstream intellectuals, accusing them of "unrestrained viciousness," and of drowning their will to power in "fatuity." The crass foulness of the 1950s and 1960s is less pervasive now, thanks to the civilizing influence of the Civil Rights movement, as well as principled opposition to the Vietnam war, and the welcome rise of feminism. Nowadays, the contribution of intellectuals is usually more subtle. Here's a small but typical example.

Political conflict in Spain

In 2016, two general elections were held in Spain. Since 1975, when dictator Francisco Franco died, Spain has been a democracy. Until 2016, two political parties basically took turns to form the government: the center-left Socialist Party (Partido Socialista Obrero Español–PSOE) and the center-right Popular Party (Partido Popular–PP). In 2016, neither party won a majority, and both of them negotiated unsuccessfully to form a coalition with smaller parties.

On August 25, our old friend the British newspaper *The Guardian* published an article about Spain (Jones 2016). The general thrust was that the Spanish public was becoming "frustrated," "weary" and "despondent" at the "squabbling" politicians, and that a third general election was an "unwelcome prospect."

Three intellectuals were quoted at length:

- Antonio Barroso, described as "an analyst at the political risk-advisory firm, Teneo Intelligence."
- Pablo Simón, a political science professor at Madrid's Carlos III University
- Emilio Sáenz-Francés, professor of history and international relations at Madrid's Comillas Pontifical University

I note in passing that the term "analyst" sounds neutral, but often is not. Teneo Intelligence says on its website that it "provides strategic counsel to CEOs [i.e. bosses–RS] and senior executives of the world's leading companies." (Teneo 2019) Hardly a hotbed of Marxism, let alone neutral. The important thing here, though, is what these experts said.

Barroso spoke of "a certain exhaustion and very little appetite for a third election," and said that the situation was "negative in the sense of the confidence of citizens in the political system."

Simón argued that "a fresh election and the attendant politicking could further alienate an already despondent electorate."

Sáenz-Francés said that the political paralysis "is damaging Spain's image around the world, but what's more worrying is that it's also damaging the already tarnished image that Spanish voters have of their politicians."

This looks like a well-founded analysis until you stop and think about it. What exactly does Sáenz-Francés mean by "Spain's image around the world?" Do you have an image of Spain? Is it damaged? And is it reasonable for Sáenz-Francés to refer to (all) Spanish voters and the "image" that they have of "their politicians?" This professor seems not to have noticed that voters tend to disagree about a lot of things. They tend to like certain politicians and dislike others. (Sorry about the truisms, but they seem to be necessary). You can't simply generalize about voters in the way he does.

Barroso talks of "the confidence of citizens in the political system?" What does that actually mean? Is there any evidence that "citizens" (many of whom—yawn—disagree about many things, just like "voters") did not have this confidence? One strong piece of evidence would be low turnout in elections in Spain compared to similar countries. But in reality, participation in recent Spanish elections has hovered at around 70 percent, compared to 65 to 69 percent in the three most recent UK general elections, and 42 to 66 percent in the latest series of US Congressional elections. Which country has the least "confidence" in its politicians?

Simón calls discussions during elections "politicking"—a derogatory term. Perhaps political debate should be called just that – "political debate," and not be trivialized.

All three commentators reinforce the assumption in the article that there is a growing divide in Spain between "voters" and "politicians," and that the voters are disillusioned with politics. Not only are such assumptions crass—"all voters" versus "all politicians" makes no sense—but they are just one way of presenting the failure of any party to form a workable majority in parliament. Millions of Spanish citizens voted for new political parties: the left-wing Podemos (We can) Party, and the centrist Ciudadanos (Citizens) Party. Perhaps this was an exciting new development, not a sign that voters were "despondent."

As well as "speaking the truth" and "exposing lies," perhaps we should expect intellectuals to:

- not use mysterious abstract notions like "the already tarnished image that Spanish voters have of their politicians."
- not use sneery language to refer to political debates.
- identify and challenge unstated assumptions, and to "lift the veil of ideology."
- not just reinforce one perspective on the world, but open up other viewpoints.

In other words, to be more like Noam Chomsky.

17. Chomsky's legacy

This chapter explores the impact of Chomsky's work in linguistics, and then floats some ideas about how to build on Chomsky's politics. I believe that Chomsky would endorse most of them, and that he would applaud my attempt to think for myself rather than just parroting his views. But he doesn't necessarily agree with them.

Linguistics

Let me start by expanding a warning from Chapter 2, Myth 8. Chomsky's approach to linguistics is a minority position within the field. Anyone who says that he is the "father" or "founder" of modern linguistics is either ignorant or mouthing platitudes.

Here's an extreme example. Jean Aitchison is an outstanding UK linguist who has written many excellent books. One of them, *Linguistics Made Easy* (Aitchison 2012), is a very good introduction to the field. The book has three pages, 19 to 21, about Chomsky, talking of his "revolution in linguistics," and calling Chomsky "arguably, the most influential linguist of the twentieth century." What she writes about his ideas is fine, but these three pages are the only references to Chomsky in the book. If Chomsky is so important and influential, why do the other 95 pages never refer to his work? If a book about classical music had two pages saying that Beethoven was the greatest composer who ever lived, but then said nothing else about him, you might wonder if the writer was just reciting a ritual.

There have, however, been some interesting developments that build on Chomsky's linguistics. The central idea in his latest work to date is that the simple computational operation called *Merge* is part of human biology. If that is correct, then linguists need to interact with biologists–particularly brain scientists, gene specialists, and evolutionary biologists–and look for biological counterparts to *Merge*. They should develop their research in parallel, so that advances in linguistics can influence work in biology, and vice versa. This interdisciplinary collaboration is sometimes called *Biolinguistics*: at the start of Chapter 10, we saw Chomsky dismissing the suggestion that this research is somehow controversial.

Some more words of warning, though. Making connections between language and the brain is part of the wider field of *cognitive neuroscience*, which links mental processes with activity in the nervous system, mainly the brain. Journalists and popular science books sometimes give the impression that recent advances in neuroscience have explained everything about human beings (or that they soon will). Chomsky is skeptical, and rightly so, in my view. He thinks that many aspects of human nature and behavior are beyond our scientific understanding, and will forever remain mysterious.

The same need for caution also applies to genetics. News reports sometimes say that "the gene for X" has been isolated, where X might be criminal tendencies or a particular disease. The reality is always more complicated. Genes don't tend to act alone, and human genetic material (the *genome*) is fantastically complex. Genetic research is making good progress, and some of the results are very important, but much work remains to be done.

Keeping these warnings in mind, there has been some good progress in linking linguistics and biology. The chapters in the 692-page *The Cambridge Handbook of Biolinguistics* (Boeckx & Grohmann 2013) are a good survey. One line of work uses *event-related potentials* (ERPs). To quote Thigpen & Keil (2017):

> The function of the human brain relies on the interactions of billions of brain cells called neurons. Neurons communicate through electrochemical processes, which change the electrical properties of the tissue in and around them. This communication is critical for human experience and

behavior. Across a wide range of scientific disciplines, researchers have therefore used recordings of neural electrical activity from the human brain to examine cognitive, emotional, and motor processes characterizing human behavior. Recordings of brain activity may also assist in clinical diagnosis and even in the treatment of brain dysfunctions.

A good way to investigate electrical properties of the human brain is to use *electroencephalography* (EEG): electrodes are placed on a person's head to detect the changes in voltage (aka electrical potential) at different places under various conditions. Unlike some other ways of measuring brain activity, EEG is non-invasive, and not too unpleasant (unlike, for example, magnetic resonance imaging [MRI] scans). Research has found that it is harmless, and that it can provide very precise information.

Voltages in the brain fluctuate all the time. By carefully placing multiple electrodes on people's heads, neuroscientists can detect larger changes in voltage, caused by thousands of neurons firing in particular areas of the brain, as humans perform specific tasks—hence the term *event-related*. A change in voltage can be *positive* or *negative*. These words have special and rather confusing meanings with electrical current: *positive* means "fewer electrons," and *negative* means "more electrons." Electrical circuits tend to return to balance, so electrons flow from the negative part to the positive part. A negative ERP just means that more electrons are generated on a particular occasion: it doesn't mean that there is less electricity circulating.

Here are three of the main language-related ERPs (based on Bornkessel-Schlesewsky & Schlesewsky 2009: 10) identified so far:

ERP	Type, and Location in the brain	Language-related feature (in mainstream theories)
N400	Negativity in the centro-parietal region	Processing the meaning of words
P600	Positivity in the centro-parietal region	Processing syntax
LAN	Negativity in the left-anterior region	Processing morphology and syntax

The "regions" are areas of the cerebral cortex, the outer layer of neural tissue that surrounds most of the brain, and that gives the brain its wrinkled appearance. The four regions are called *lobes* (rounded bits that stick out), and you can see where they are in fig 1. (The "anterior" region is another name for the "frontal" region).

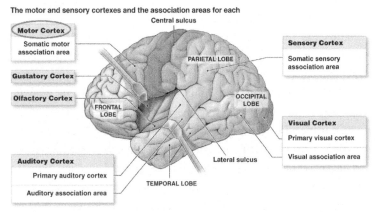

Fig 1: Regions of the Cerebral cortex (Source: https://socratic.org/questions/in-what-lobe-is-the-somatic-motor-cortex-located-in-the-brain [Creative Commons license])

Bornkessel-Schlesewsky & Schlesewsky argue in their 2009 book that a direct link between these ERPS and the language features has become less certain as research has advanced. They propose more complex relationships within the brain.

You may recall from Chapter 12 that children acquiring English as their first language often go through a stage where they "regularize" past tense forms, saying things like *bringed, comed* and *speaked,* even though they never hear adults saying these words. Biolinguists have explored the possibility that regular and irregular morphological processes (processes that modify words) take place in different parts of the brain. In a group of experiments with regular and irregular verbs in English, German and Spanish, they found that the brain activated differently, and in different places, with regular and irregular verbs. Bornkessel-Schlesewsky & Schlesewsky (2009: 57-66) review some of this research and again propose more complex links.

Returning to *Merge,* things perhaps look more positive. Bornkessel-Schlesewsky & Schlesewsky review a range of recent work and suggest that "the only syntactic operation which appears to have possible neurobiological correlates is Merge or something akin to it." (Schlesewsky & Bornkessel-Schlesewsky 2013: 279) They focus on the "time problem": for Chomsky, *Merge* is not a process that takes place in real time but a computational model of language in the mind. The neurobiological counterpart to *Merge,* on the other hand, has to include a theory about how it operates in real time. The authors survey several proposed solutions to this problem and are confident that the problem can be solved.

Biolinguistics is a young field, and still relatively small. But it is an exciting field, with many different theories being proposed and discussed. Chomsky's legacy in linguistics is bearing some promising fruit.

Politics

I will start by repeating another warning. There is no essential connection between Chomsky's linguistics and his political activism (see Myth 7 in Chapter 2). Yes, both of them challenge conventional wisdom. Both of them are based on evidence. But Chomsky's linguistics tries to be scientific—he thinks of it as part of the science of biology. Science is sometimes complicated and very hard. If you want to make sense of it, you need to study, read, gather data, experiment, and, ideally, work alongside experts. Political activism is not complicated. It doesn't require extensive study or special expertise. More important are courage, firm principles, a sense of humor, optimism, and the ability to listen. It is positively harmful, in my view, to give the impression that you need to study any body of scientific writing in order to contribute to justice and freedom in the world. Chomsky has emphasized that point many times.

Some of the politics chapters in this book have dealt with specific parts of the world, such as Korea and the Middle East. Chomsky has often spoken about these regions, and they are currently important flashpoints where the US is an obstacle to peace and justice. Other chapters have dealt with urgent threats to human survival, notably nuclear war and the climate crisis, where the US government and its corporate allies are leading us into an abyss.

What can you, dear reader, do about these problems? If you live in the US or another democratic country where you and other like-minded people can vote out the government and replace it with a better one, you have essentially two choices:

1. Join a political party that has a chance of gaining power and is closest to your views. Right now, that probably means the Democrats in the US and the Labour Party in the UK.
2. Do something else.

Let's look at these two alternatives carefully. The first one is, at the time of writing, a live topic for many people. In the US Democratic Party and the British Labour Party, powerful people conspire tenaciously, and often viciously, to keep the party near the "center" ground. For people who desperately want radical political change, like Chomsky and the present writer, the traditional left-of-center parties do not look too promising at present. Should you stay, or join, and try to change a political party so it can be a genuine force for change?

Political parties—for and against

Let's look at some good reasons for working for change within large, established political parties. Most importantly, they offer a route to power. They have resources, including paid workers, buildings, money, and millions of supporters. They have connections to trade unions, who also have resources, and who are surely crucial in social change. Political parties are where the action is. The alternative is to be just a voice shouting impotently in the wilderness: as the late English comedian Jeremy Hardy once said, you can instead spend the rest of your life shouting "bastards" at the TV news. Or as the old saying goes, "An unorganized socialist is a contradiction in terms." If you want a world where people cooperate, and we care about everyone, then cutting yourself off is a large step in the wrong direction.

There are some fantastic people in the US Democratic Party, the British Labour Party, and similar organizations throughout the world. Many of them work tirelessly at the grassroots, giving up much of their free time and expecting no recognition or reward. Some of them are prominent figures. Alexandria Ocasio-Cortez, a member of Congress for part of New York City, says that "in a modern, moral, and wealthy society, no American should be too poor to live," and she seems to mean it. She is young, articulate, tenacious, and witty. Her "Green New Deal" offers a way to change the economy and avoid climate catastrophe. Labour members of the UK parliament like Rebecca Long-Bailey and John McDonnell have similar inspiring qualities, and they also propose a just transition to a green economy. They have supported a Universal Basic Income, which would guarantee that every person in the UK has their basic needs met—enough money to have a place to live, enough to eat, and health care.

Large political parties get media coverage—not always positive, of course, but they are in the news. We need, very urgently, to replace dangerous bullies like Donald Trump and Boris Johnson with better political leaders. This means working, and voting, for the organizations that have a chance of doing this. Chomsky has said that he will vote for the Democrat candidate in the 2020 presidential election.

So what are the reasons not to sign up? Most obviously, these parties are coalitions of people with a wide range of different views, often opposed to mine. Some of these people hate progressive and liberal individuals like me with virulent loathing. Years ago, I spoke at a meeting in my hometown, which was supposed to build bridges between the Labour Right and socialists like me. It was not a lot of fun: the verbal abuse from the Right was vitriolic, and if looks could kill, I would be long dead. The only people who have directed so much hatred at me personally were fascists in the National Front and the British National Party. Is it possible to rescue the Democratic and Labour Parties?

As we noted in the opening chapters, much of Chomsky's political activism has been directed against the liberal end of the mainstream spectrum. These are the people who set the boundaries for acceptable political debate, and they have also committed terrible atrocities: it was the Democrat Presidents Kennedy and Johnson who escalated the murderous US assault on Indochina. It was the UK Labour Party that joined the disastrous invasion of Iraq in 2003, applauded the bombing of a radio station in Belgrade in 1999 (cf. Chapter 5), and supplied former MPs for the boards of arms companies, as I pointed out in Chapter 4. Barack Obama happily expanded oil production in the US, described by Chomsky as "an eloquent death-knell for the species" (see Chapter 9), and pursued brave whistleblowers like Chelsea Manning and Edward Snowden.

Working within mainstream political parties can be very boring. Party meetings are often full of tedious procedural business, necessary at times and beloved by some activists but felt by many others to be eroding their brains. In my family, we like to parody party bureaucracy with a recurrent joke about "voting to suspend standing orders" after dinner. More seriously, working for piecemeal reforms, constantly compromising with businesspeople, and regularly being encouraged to scale down your ambitions so that you are "realistic" and "electable," takes a toll: you can start to believe this type of thinking and become cynical and joyless—in short, you may turn into the type of person you joined the party to challenge.

So that's one choice. Lots of people are working hard to remove dangerous bullies like Donald Trump and Boris Johnson from power. Should you join them?

Alternatives

Or you can choose the other alternative, doing something else. You probably want a little more detail, so here are some thoughts. You could devote yourself to eliminating one of the big dangers that Chomsky regularly emphasizes: nuclear devastation or climate catastrophe. Find the best group you can which is trying to avert these dangers, and join up: perhaps the International Campaign to Abolish Nuclear Weapons on the first one, and 350.org on the second. Check them out, see what actions they take and who supports them. Use your skills, time, energy, and money to build up these organizations and increase their impact.

You could decide that a major obstacle to radical change is the demonization of immigrants and refugees, based on the pernicious and divisive belief that "Some humans ain't human" in the words of the late singer John Prine. You could go further and decide that nationalism, and indeed national borders, are ludicrous relics of a bygone age, and that future generations (if there are any) will look back on these relics as we look back on slavery—with disgust.

You could take as your starting point the Universal Declaration of Human Rights (UDHR), adopted by the United Nations in 1948. Chomsky devoted a book to the UDHR on its 50th anniversary (Chomsky 1999b). If we believe that all humans, regardless of their ethnic, religious, and cultural background, have the same basic rights, then we should trumpet that loud and clear. Not only is this the right thing to do, but it also creates a platform for common cause between political activists and religious people, many of whom believe that God does not discriminate between people on the basis of ethnic origin, skin color, or nationality.

Or you can put your energy into a small-scale, local campaign. Here's an example. Brighton, where I live, is famous for its beach, which has lots of stones and very little sand. Disabled people can look at the beach from the footpath nearby, but are almost entirely unable to walk on it and be close to the sea. One woman, Claire Nelson, has made it her mission to make Brighton beach accessible to everyone. She says that several seaside towns around the world put down temporary boardwalks for wheelchairs in the summer and have developed creative solutions for a range of disabilities. The local newspaper recently reported that her tireless work is beginning to get results (Booker-Lewis 2020). The great thing about local campaigns is that they sometimes succeed, and you can see change happening.

Back to Chomsky

Or you can think about more fundamental issues. If you agree with Chomsky that structures of power and domination must be challenged and dismantled, and that we need an "Independent Left" to pursue that agenda, then go ahead and contribute. What needs to be done?

Chomsky has often spoken about education, as we saw in Chapter 3. We need more people who don't tolerate injustice and become active champions for change. It is starting to happen, with young women like Malala Yousafzai and Greta Thunberg taking the lead. As someone memorably said, "When leaders behave like children, it is time for children to behave like leaders."

Reforming education is a vital part of empowering young people. Mostly, that is about removing barriers to their natural curiosity and resisting the constant attacks on real education from the right. Rote learning, testing, and undermining public education have been a constant priority for mainstream politicians for as long as I can remember. This is a crucial terrain of class conflict, if you will forgive the vulgar-Marxist jargon, and every victory is important.

It isn't just schooling: our entire approach to young people should be based on respect and support—and then getting out of their way when they steamroller joyously through the oppressive structures which dominate our world. Older people, particularly parents and teachers, need to encourage curiosity, disrespect for illegitimate authority, playfulness, creativity, and courage. (Note that parents are NOT to blame: expecting two people to be sole caretakers while they also struggle to make a living is cruel and unworkable: again, future generations will probably be aghast that we take it for granted.)

An essential first step is to make it illegal for adults to use violence against young people. More and more countries are doing this, and it must happen everywhere. The organization *Children are Unbeatable* will tell you more. Criminalizing adult violence should go alongside support for parents and teachers, so they can change their ways.

Looking back now at Chapter 4, we saw that for Chomsky, anarchism is about challenging illegitimate authority, and extending democracy to every area of social and economic life. The link with education is this: we should design teaching and learning so that they help young people to take the lead and show us the way. The movement for change should be non-violent, of course, but also diverse, messy, and unpredictable. It will make us old-timers feel uncomfortable at times. It will have to be tough enough to stand up to the vicious attacks from established power that will rain down when that power feels threatened. It won't always be fun, and sometimes it will be dull or dangerous. The movement will need to build up strong bonds of solidarity to endure despite the bad times.

What about Chapter 5, where we talked about Chomsky's consistent drive to expose and counteract "propaganda?" Remember also his troubling claim in Chapter 3 that educated people are most indoctrinated: they create the propaganda, and they come to believe it. You could devote your energy to continuing this part of Chomsky's work. In the UK, *Media Lens* is one (small) organization that does this, with the explicit aim of following Chomsky's lead. This is an exciting area, where you will find great people to work with. You can support, or create, alternative news sources, and try to change (or dismantle) some of the worst mainstream media. This doesn't need special intelligence or study. It's more like cleaning out our minds and unlearning rubbish that we have taken for granted.

The choice before you is whether to build a good political *party*, or to be part of a more diffuse *movement*. If you can do both, that's great. Just remember to take care of yourself and the people close to you while you do it.

Two final thoughts

Firstly, if you live in a rich, democratic country, where established power is usually not brutal, you are immensely privileged. The possibilities for useful political action are many, and the personal cost to you is less likely to be devastating than it is in many parts of the world. Chomsky often makes these points, while also emphasizing that privileged people need to be inspired by those who are less fortunate: the labor organizers, human rights defenders, environmental activists, and opponents of exploitation, poverty, racism, and sexism in the poor parts of the world. Against overwhelming odds, and often at great personal cost, these people are in the front line of the battle for a better world. We need to follow their lead.

Secondly, if any part of this chapter is helpful, then I am glad, but it is important that you think for yourself. Chomsky saw the value of that at a young age, and he has done it all his life. You can contribute to his legacy by doing the same.

Endnotes

Chapter 1 – Chomsky's Life

1. On a personal note: I do not think many publications about language are worth reading every year or so for sheer pleasure, but Chomsky's 1959 review of Skinner is one of them. I take a similar view of Chomsky's "Objectivity and Liberal Scholarship," available as a chapter in Chomsky (1967) and also as a stand-alone book (Chomsky 2003b): not for pleasure in this case (reading about the crushing of the Spanish revolution in the 1930s is heartbreaking), but for the liberating effect on my mind.

Chapter 2 – Myths

1. Here's another example of Chomsky poking fun at elite opinions. Pointless sarcasm or justified irony? You be the judge:

> Consider political commentator Michael Kinsley, who represents "the left" in mainstream commentary and television debate. When the State Department publicly confirmed U.S. support for terrorist attacks on agricultural cooperatives in Nicaragua, Kinsley wrote that we should not be too quick to condemn this official policy. Such international terrorist operations doubtless cause "vast civilian suffering," he conceded. But if they succeed "to undermine morale and confidence in the government," then they may be "perfectly legitimate." The policy is "sensible" if "cost-benefit analysis" shows that "the amount of blood and misery that will be poured in" yields "democracy," in

the conventional sense already discussed. [Elites decide, the poor do as they are told–RS]

As a spokesman for the establishment left, Kinsley insists that terror must meet the pragmatic criterion; violence should not be employed for its own sake, merely because we find it amusing. This more humane conception would readily be accepted by Saddam Hussein, Abu Nidal, and the Hizbullah kidnappers, who, presumably, also consider terror pointless unless it is of value for their ends. These facts help us situate enlightened Western opinion on the international spectrum. (Chomsky 1991: 377)

Chapter 5 – Propaganda

1. Here's another example of how the world's media focus on atrocities committed by "them" but not those by "us"–exactly the opposite of what they should do in Chomsky's view, as we noted under Myth 5 in Chapter 1. The slaughter of twelve French journalists in the *Charlie Hebdo* attack of 2015 was covered extensively and denounced (rightly) as appalling. The slaughter of sixteen people in the NATO bombing of Serbian TV headquarters in 1999 was hailed as "entirely justified" and "legitimate" by UK Prime Minister Tony Blair and US military spokespeople. It has been almost entirely forgotten. See Quinn (2019) for a rare exception.

Chapter 6 – Korea

1. One of these was a State Department memorandum of April 1944 called "Petroleum Policy of the United States" (Chomsky 1987: 6). Another was 'National Security Council Memorandum 68' (Chomsky 1985: 198).

Chapter 10 – Democracy in America

1. Democrat candidates in US presidential elections suffer from a systematically unfair electoral system. Both Al Gore in 2000 and Hillary Clinton in 2016 won many more votes nationwide than their Republican opponents. They lost the election because of the "Electoral College" system, which gives all the college votes in each state to the candidate with a majority in that state. A partisan Secretary of State in Florida, and a biased Supreme Court, also played a part in the election of George Bush junior in 2000.

2. The nearest UK equivalent is perhaps Conservative politicians who invoke Winston Churchill, an alcoholic racist who sent troops to fire on striking miners, allegedly suggested "Keep Britain white" as a campaign slogan in the 1950s, and was such a beloved war hero that in 1945 he was immediately voted out of office by a landslide. More George Custer than Will Kane.

Chapter 12 – Universal Grammar

1. Running differs from walking because it includes a phase when both feet are off the ground (called "floating" by kinesiologists). If you didn't already know that, then you've definitely learned something from reading this book.

Chapter 14 – Meaning

1. A "property" is a feature or characteristic of something. Garlic is said to have healing properties. Garlic also has the following

properties: it is a round white vegetable, it has small sections called *cloves*, and people add it to food for a strong pleasant flavor (thanks, *Macmillan Dictionary*). Garlic has the further properties of having a very strong taste if you eat it raw, of rendering those who eat it raw terribly malodorous, and (in some superstitions) of protecting you against vampires.

Chapter 15 – Evolution

1. A third possibility is put forward in the book and film 2001: A *Space Odyssey*: some benevolent advanced aliens rewired our ancestors' brains using a mysterious black monolith. I like this idea, fanciful though it is.

2. The idea of a malevolent advanced civilization—for example, the alien invaders in the film *Independence Day*—is very implausible for precisely that reason. Groups of heavily-armed malevolent organisms have a natural tendency to destroy themselves: they can only flourish if their ability to co-operate outweighs their malevolence.

3. The book and film 2001 suggested that the ability to fight better was crucial to the survival of the lucky few hominins whose brains were rewired by aliens. That's good drama, but not necessarily good science.

Sources

Aitchison, J. 2012. *Linguistics made easy*. London, Hodder Education.

Allott, N., C. Knight and N. Smith. 2019 (eds.). *The Responsibility of Intellectuals: Reflections by Noam Chomsky and others after 50 years*. London, UCL Press. Free to download from https://www.uclpress.co.uk/products/123963.

Amnesty International. 2018. The Hooded Men: torture, lies and a quest for justice. https://www.amnesty.org.uk/hooded-men-torture-uk-ireland.

Bartlett, N. 2018. Jeremy Corbyn strengthens his hold on Labour as the party appoints Unite veteran Jennie Formby as general secretary. *Daily Mirror*, 20 March 2018. https://www.mirror.co.uk/news/politics/corbyn-strengthens-hold-labour-party-12221476.

BBC News. 2002. Chomsky publisher cleared in Turkey. http://news.bbc.co.uk/1/hi/world/europe/1817598.stm.

BDS (Boycott, Divestment, Sanctions) 2017. Chomsky clarifies position on the cultural boycott of Israel. https://bdsmovement.net/news/chomsky-clarifies-position-cultural-boycott-israel.

Boeckx, C. & M. Grohman (eds.). 2013. *The Cambridge Handbook of Biolinguistics*. Cambridge, CUP.

Booker-Lewis, S. 2020. Help for disabled people to use Brighton beach on the way. *The Argus*, 4 March 2020. Online: https://www.theargus.co.uk/news/18279485.help-disabled-people-use-brighton-beach-way/.

Bornkessel-Schlesewsky, I. & M. Schlesewsky. 2009. *Processing Syntax and Morphology: A Neurocognitive Perspective*. Oxford, OUP.

Brockes, E. 2005. The Greatest Intellectual? Noam Chomsky interviewed by Emma Brockes. *The Guardian*, 31 October 2005. Online (with comments by Chomsky) at: https://chomsky.info/20051031/

Brown, A. 2003. A way with words – an interview with Larry Trask. *The Guardian*, 26 June 2003. Online at: https://www.theguardian.com/science/2003/jun/26/ scienceinterviews.artsandhumanities

Bulletin of the Atomic Scientists. 2019. The Doomsday Clock. https://thebulletin.org/doomsday-clock/

Cammaerts, M.-C. 2014. Performance of the Species-Typical Alarm Response in Young Workers of the Ant *Myrmica sabuleti* (Hymenoptera: Formicidae) Is Induced by Interactions with Mature Workers. *Journal of Insect Science* 14 (234), 1-6. https://academic.oup.com/jinsectscience/article-pdf/doi/ 10.1093/jisesa/ieu096/25454022/ieu096.pdf.

Chandler, D. 2009. Climate change odds much worse than thought. New analysis shows warming could be double previous estimates. MIT News Office, May 19, 2009. http://news.mit.edu/ 2009/roulette-0519

Chomsky, N. 1957. *Syntactic Structures*. The Hague, Mouton.

Chomsky, N. 1959. Review of B. F. Skinner, *Verbal Behaviour*. *Language*, 35:1, 26-58. Online at: http://pds21.egloos.com/pds/ 201407/08/38/ Review_of_Verbal_BF_Skinners_Verbal_Behavior.pdf. Reprinted in J. Fodor & J Katz (eds.), *The structure of language: Readings in the philosophy of language* (Englewood Cliffs, NJ, Prentice Hall, 1964), 547–78. Also reprinted in L.A. Jakobovits and M.S. Miron (eds.), *Readings in the Psychology of Language* (New York, NY, Prentice-Hall, 1967), 142-172 (The preface to this reprint is online at: http://www.cogprints.org/1148/1/chomsky.htm). Also reprinted in A. Arnove (ed.), *The Essential Chomsky* (London, Bodley Head, 2008), 1-30.

Chomsky, N. 1964. *Current Issues in Linguistic Theory*. The Hague, Mouton. Reprinted in J. Fodor & J Katz (eds.), *The structure of language: Readings in the philosophy of language* (Englewood Cliffs, NJ, Prentice Hall, 1964), 50-118.

Chomsky, N. 1969a. *American Power and the New Mandarins*. Harmondsworth, Penguin.

Chomsky, N. 1969b. The responsibility of intellectuals. In Chomsky (1969a: 256-290).

Chomsky, N. 1982. *Towards a New Cold War: Essays on the Current Crisis and how We Got There*. New York, NY., Pantheon.

Chomsky, N. 1985. *Turning The Tide: US Intervention in Central America and the Struggle for Peace*. Boston, MA., South End Press.

Chomsky, N. 1987. *On Power and Ideology; The Managua Lectures*. Boston, MA., South End Press.

Chomsky, N. 1988. *Language and Problems of Knowledge: The Managua Lectures*, Cambridge, MA, MIT Press.

Chomsky, N. 1989. *Necessary Illusions: Thought Control in Democratic Societies*. London, Pluto Press.

Chomsky, N. 1991. *Deterring Democracy*. Boston, MA, South End Press.

Chomsky, N. 1994. *Secrets, lies and democracy. Interviews with David Barsamian*. Tucson, AZ., Odonian Press.

Chomsky N. 1995. Language and Nature. *Mind* 104 (413): 1–61.

Chomsky, N. 1996. *Class Warfare: Interviews with David Barsamian*. London, Pluto Press.

Chomsky, N. 1997. *Media control: the spectacular achievements of propaganda*. New York, NY, Seven Stories Press.

Chomsky, N. 1999a. *The Fateful Triangle: The United States, Israel, and the Palestinians*. London, Pluto Press.

Chomsky, N. 1999b. *The Umbrella of U.S. power: the universal declaration of human rights and the contradictions of U.S. Policy*. New York, NY, Seven Stories Press.

Chomsky, N. 2000a. *New Horizons in the Study of Language and Mind*. 2nd Edn. Cambridge, Cambridge University Press.

Chomsky, N. 2000b. *Chomsky on Miseducation*. Edited by D. Macedo. Oxford, Rowman & Littlefield.

Chomsky, N. 2002. *On Nature and Language*. Cambridge, Cambridge University Press.

Chomsky, N. 2003a. *Media Control: The spectacular achievements of propaganda*. New York, NY., Seven Stories Press.

Chomsky, N. 2003b. *Objectivity and Liberal Scholarship*. New York,

NY, The Free Press. (Earlier published as the first chapter of Chomsky 1969a). Also republished in part in Peck, J. (ed.), *The Chomsky Reader* (London, Serpents Tail, 1988), 83-120. Full text online at: http://www.ditext.com/chomsky/1968.html.

Chomsky, N. 2005a. Open Letter to *The Guardian*. [Not published in *The Guardian*]. https://chomsky.info/20051113/.

Chomsky, N. 2005b. *Imperial Ambitions: Interviews with David Barsamian*. London, Hamish Hamilton.

Chomsky, N. 2007. *What we say goes: Conversations on US power in a changing world with David Barsamian*. London, Allen & Unwin.

Chomsky, N. 2008. *Interventions*. Harmondsworth, Penguin.

Chomsky, N. 2010a. Some simple evo-devo theses: How true might they be for language? In R. Larson, V. Deprez, & H. Yamakido, (eds.), *The Evolution of Human Language: Biolinguistic perspectives* (Cambridge, Cambridge University Press), 45- 62.

Chomsky, N. 2010b. Afterword. In R. Ehrlich, *Conversations with Terrorists* (Boulder, CO, Paradigm Press), 151-4.

Chomsky, N. 2012. *Making the Future: Occupations, Interventions, Empire and Resistance*. San Francisco, CA., City Lights Books.

Chomsky, N. 2013. *Power systems: Conversations on global democratic uprisings and the new challenges to US Empire. Interviews with David Barsamian*. New York, NY., Henry Holt.

Chomsky, N. 2014a. *Democracy and Power. The Delhi Lectures*. Cambridge, Open Book Publishers.

Chomsky, N. 2014b. Security and State Power: The Prospects for Survival. https://chomsky.info/20140303/

Chomsky, N. 2015a. *Masters of Mankind: Essays and Lectures, 1969-2013*. Harmondsworth, Penguin.

Chomsky, N. 2015b. *On Power and Ideology; The Managua Lectures*. (2nd edn). Chicago, IL., Haymarket Books.

Chomsky, N. 2016. *What kind of creatures are we?* New York, NY., Columbia University Press.

Chomsky, N. 2019. Interview with Andy Heintz. In A. Heintz (ed.), *Dissidents of the International Left* (Oxford, New Internationalist Publications), 25-30.

Chomsky, N. & G. Achcar. 2007. *Perilous Power*. London, Penguin Books.

Chomsky, N. & D. Barsamian. 2007. *What We Say Goes: U.S. Power in a Changing World*. Crows Nest, NSW, Australia, Allen & Unwin.

Chomsky, N. & D. Barsamian. 2017. *Global Discontents: Conversations on the Rising Threats to Democracy*. New York, NY., Metropolitan Books.

Chomsky, N. & E. Herman. 1979. *After the Cataclysm, Postwar Indochina and the Reconstruction of Imperial ideology*. Boston, MA., South End Press.

Chomsky, N. & C. Polychroniou. 2017. *Optimism Over Despair*. Harmondsworth, Penguin.

Chomsky, N. & R. Pollin. 2020. *Climate Crisis and the Global Green New Deal: The Political Economy of Saving the Planet*. New York, NY., & London, Verso.

Chomsky, W. 1957. *Hebrew: The Eternal Language*. Philadelphia, PA., Jewish Publication Society of America.

Cohen, J. & J. Rogers. 1991. Knowledge, Morality and Hope: the Social Thought of Noam Chomsky. *New Left Review* 187 (May-June 1991): 5-27. https://newleftreview.org/issues/I187/articles/joshua-cohen-joel-rogers-knowledge-morality-and-hope-the-social-thought-of-noam-chomsky. Also at: https://libcom.org/library/knowledge-morality-and-hope-the-social-thought-of-noam-chomsky-by-joshua-cohen-and-joel-rogers, and https://www.cows.org/knowledge-morality-and-hope-the-social-thought-of-noam-chomsky.

Collier, P. & D. Horowitz (eds.). 2004. *The Anti Chomsky Reader*. New York, NY., Encounter Books.

Cumings, B. 2010. *The Korean War: A History*. New York, NY., Random House.

Deutsche Welle. 2020. An ongoing crisis: Freedom of speech in Turkey. https://www.dw.com/en/an-ongoing-crisis-freedom-of-speech-in-turkey/a-47405671.

Dewey, J. 1986. Experience and Education. *The Educational Forum*, 50:3, 241-252. (Extracts from Dewey's book of the same name,

published in 1938). The full book is online at: https://ruby.fgcu.edu/
Courses/ndemers/Colloquium/ExperiencEducationDewey.pdf.

Dixon, K. C. Linney, M. Paukovic & A. Watson. 2018. Out of the
shadows: Promoting Openness and Accountability in the Global
Defence Industry. London, Transparency International.
https://www.transparency.org.uk/publications/out-of-the-
shadows/.

Dunbar, R. 2012. Gossip and the social origins of language. In
Tallerman & Gibson (2012): 343-345.

Edemariam, A. 2013. Noam Chomsky: 'No individual changes
anything alone'. The Guardian, 22 March 2013.:
https://www.theguardian.com/world/2013/mar/22/noam-
chomsky-no-individual-changes-anything-alone.

Egret, E. 2017. The Revolving Door Between the Government &
the Arms Trade. London, Stop the War Coalition.
http://www.stopwar.org.uk/index.php/news-comment/
2720-the-revolving-door-between-the-government-the-arms-
trade.

Encyclopaedia Britannica. 2019. Bloody Sunday. Northern Ireland
1972. https://www.britannica.com/event/Bloody-Sunday-
Northern-Ireland-1972

Gray, B. Now you see it, now you don't: Chomsky's Reflections.
Forum Linguisticum 2, 1977/78, 65-74.

Greenpeace. 2019. ExxonMobil Climate Denial Funding 1998-2014.
https://exxonsecrets.org/html/

Greenwald, G. 2013. How Noam Chomsky is discussed. The
Guardian, 23 March 2013. https://www.theguardian.com/
commentisfree/2013/mar/23/noam-chomsky-guardian-
personality.

Halle, J. & N. Chomsky. 2016. An Eight Point Brief for LEV (Lesser
Evil Voting). https://chomsky.info/an-eight-point-brief-for-lev-
lesser-evil-voting/.

Harris, Z. 1951. Methods in Structural Linguistics. Chicago, IL.,
University of Chicago Press.

Herman, E. & N. Chomsky. 1988. Manufacturing Consent: The

Political Economy of the Mass Media. New York, NY., Pantheon Books.

Hockett, C. 1968. *The state of the art.* The Hague, Mouton.

Home Stratosphere. 2019. 43 Types of Tables for Your Home (Buying Guide). https://www.homestratosphere.com/tables/.

ICAN (International Campaign to Abolish Nuclear Weapons) 2019. Nuclear arsenals. https://www.icanw.org/nuclear_arsenals

Jones, S. 2016. Spain braces itself for unwanted gift on Christmas Day: a third election. The *Guardian*, 25 August 2016. https://www.theguardian.com/world/2016/aug/25/spain-mariano-rajoy-third-general-election-christmas-day

Karlin, S. 2017. Chilling PBS Documentary Recounts The Nuclear Accident That Nearly Destroyed Arkansas. https://www.fastcompany.com/3066918/chilling-pbs-doc-recounts-the-nuclear-accident-that-nearly-destroyed-arkansas.

Lee, S. 2015. The Japanese Empire at War, 1931- 1945. In R. Overy (ed.), *The Oxford Illustrated History of World War Two* (Oxford, Oxford University Press), 35-73.

Lukin, A. 2011. The paradox of Noam Chomsky on language and power. http://theconversation.com/the-paradox-of-noam-chomsky-on-language-and-power-4174

MacFarquhar, L. 2003. The Devil's Accountant. Noam Chomsky's criticism of America's role in the world has increased his isolation—and his audience. *New Yorker*, 31 March 2003. https://www.newyorker.com/magazine/2003/03/31/the-devils-accountant

Miller, D. 2017. Leaving by the Back Door: Priti Patel and the crisis of corruption. Bath, University of Bath. http://blogs.bath.ac.uk/iprblog/2017/11/10/leaving-by-the-back-door-priti-patel-and-the-crisis-of-corruption/.

Minnich, E. 2006. Dewey's Philosophy of Life. In D.T. Hansen (ed.), *John Dewey and Our Educational Prospect* (Albany, NY, State University of New York Press), 147-164.

Mitchell, P. & J. Schoeffel (eds.). 2002. *Understanding Power: The Indispensable Chomsky.* New York, NY., The New Press.

Mullen, A. 2009. The Propaganda Model after 20 Years: Interview with Edward S. Herman and Noam Chomsky. Online at: https://chomsky.info/200911__/.

New York Times. 2019. $129 Billion Puerto Rico Bankruptcy Plan Could Be Model for States. https://www.nytimes.com/2019/09/27/business/puerto-rico-bankruptcy-promesa.html.

Otero, C. (ed.). 2003. *Chomsky on Democracy and Education*. New York, NY., Routledge Falmer.

Perlo-Freeman, S. 2016. Transparency and accountability in military spending. Stockholm, SIPRI (Stockholm International Peace Research Institute). https://sipri.org/commentary/topical-backgrounder/2016/transparency-and-accountability-military-spending.

Plimer, I. 2009. *Heaven and Earth: Global Warming, the Missing Science*. Ballan, Australia, Connorcourt Publishing.

Quinn, S. 2019. Forgotten War Crimes: NATO's 1999 Attack on Serbia's State TV Headquarters 'Wiped from the Record'. https://www.globalresearch.ca/forgotten-war-crimes-natos-1999-attack-serbias-state-tv-headquarters/5625469.

Rai, M. 1995. *Chomsky's Politics*. London, Verso.

Révész, G. 2015. *Introduction to Formal Languages*. North Chelmsford, MA., Courier Corporation.

Richardson, J. 2007. *Analysing Newspapers: An Approach from Critical Discourse Analysis*. London, Palgrave MacMillan.

Riemer, N. 2010. *Introducing semantics*. Cambridge, CUP.

Salkie, R. 1990/2015. *The Chomsky update: linguistics and politics*. London, Unwin Hyman. (Reissued 2015 in Routledge Library Editions).

Schlesewsky, M. & I. Bornkessel-Schlesewsky. 2013. Computational primitives in syntax and possible brain correlates. In Boeckx & Grohman (2013), 257-282.

Slabakova, R. 2013. What is easy and what is hard in second language acquisition: A generative perspective. In M. García Mayo, M. Gutierrez-Mangado, & M. Martínez Adrián (eds.), *Contemporary*

Approaches to Second Language Acquisition (Amsterdam, John Benjamins), 5-28.

Smith, N. & N. Allott. 2016. *Chomsky: Ideas and Ideals* (3rd edn.). Cambridge, Cambridge University Press.

Smith, N. & A. Smith. 2019. Reflections on Chomsky's 'The Responsibility of Intellectuals'. In Allott, Knight & Smith (2019), 7-25.

Sontag, D. 1999. Orthodox Confront U.S. Reform Rabbis at Western Wall. *New York Times*, 2 Feb 1999. https://www.nytimes.com/1999/02/02/world/orthodox-confront-us-reform-rabbis-at-western-wall.html

Sperlich, W. 2006. *Noam Chomsky*. London, Reaktion Books.

Stuckler D., L. King & S. Basu. 2008. International Monetary Fund programs and tuberculosis outcomes in post-communist countries. *PLoS Med* 5(7): e143. https://journals.plos.org/plosmedicine/article?id=10.1371/journal.pmed.0050143.

Tallerman, N. 2014. No syntax saltation in language evolution. *Language Sciences* 46: 207-219.

Tallerman, M. & K. Gibson (eds.). 2012. *The Oxford Handbook of Language Evolution*. Oxford, Oxford University Press.

Tattersall, I. 2017. How can we detect when language emerged? *Psychonomic Bulletin & Review* 24.2: 64-67. https://link.springer.com/article/10.3758/s13423-016-1075-9.

Tejada, C. 2017. Money, Power, Family: Inside South Korea's Chaebol. *New York Times*, Feb. 17, 2017. https://www.nytimes.com/2017/02/17/business/south-korea-chaebol-samsung.html

Teneo. 2019. Teneo is the global CEO advisory firm. https://www.teneo.com/our-firm/.

Thigpen, N.N. & A. Keil, 2017. Event-Related Potentials. *Reference Module in Neuroscience and Biobehavioral Psychology*. Amsterdam, Elsevier. Online: http://dx.doi.org/10.1016/B978-0-12-809324-5.02456-1.

Vaughan, C. 2003. Theories of bipedal walking: an odyssey. *Journal of Biomechanics* 36: 513-523.

Weisbrot, M. 2019. The Scandal of Puerto Rico's Botched Disaster

Relief. https://zcomm.org/znetarticle/the-scandal-of-puerto-ricos-botched-disaster-relief/.

World Peace Foundation, 2015. Cambodia: U.S. bombing, civil war, & Khmer Rouge. https://sites.tufts.edu/atrocityendings/2015/08/07/cambodia-u-s-bombing-civil-war-khmer-rouge/

Zickfeld, K., S. Solomon, S. & D. Gilford, D. 2017. Centuries of thermal sea-level rise due to anthropogenic emissions of short-lived greenhouse gases. *Proceedings of the National Academy of Sciences* 114.4, January 24, 2017: 657–662. https://www.pnas.org/content/114/4/657.short.

Suggested Reading

By Chomsky

For Chomsky's own words, look at the website www.chomsky.info. Just about all you need is there. YouTube also has many talks by Chomsky, as well as interviews with him.

Another good place to start is any book of interviews with Chomsky by his admirable friend David Barsamian: recent ones include *What we say goes* (2007), *Power Systems* (2013), and *Global Discontents* (2017).

Chomsky's 2016 book *What kind of creatures are we?* is a gentle introduction to his current thinking about language and evolution, with a short chapter about his political views. A timely book by Chomsky and Robert Pollin, *Climate Crisis and the Global Green New Deal: The Political Economy of Saving the Planet*, came out in 2020 (Chomsky & Pollin 2020).

In my view, two of Chomsky's most important books are these:

- *Objectivity and Liberal Scholarship*. (Chomsky 2003b).

This short book, written in the early 1960s, pours scorn on intellectuals who unthinkingly support the status quo. Chomsky unmasks their hidden assumptions about US policy in Indochina and then discusses at length a book about the Spanish Civil War, which he describes as "an excellent example of liberal scholarship." He shows how the author's elitist views distort his account of the anarchist-inspired popular revolution which took place in much of Spain. The revolution was crushed by Spanish Communists before being finally defeated by Franco and his fascist army. It's a compelling read. (See the "Sources" chapter for various ways to access this text).

- (With Edward Herman) *Manufacturing Consent: The Political Economy of the Mass Media*. (Herman & Chomsky 1988).

This excellent book is the most comprehensive account of the 'Propaganda Model', which claims that the mass media systematically serve as champions for elite ideology (see chapter 5 for more). The detailed examples are, of course, rather dated now, but the general principles still hold. For a more recent assessment by Herman & Chomsky, take a look at Mullen (2009), available online.

About Chomsky

For Chomsky's life, Wolfgang Sperlich's *Noam Chomsky* (Sperlich 2006) is thorough and readable.

The best and most comprehensive book about Chomsky's thinking is *Chomsky: Ideas and Ideals* by Neil Smith and Nicholas Allott (Smith & Allott 2016).

Milan Rai's *Chomsky's Politics* (Rai 1995), though a little dated, is excellent.

Joshua Cohen and Joel Rogers wrote a good article in 1991 called "Knowledge, Morality and Hope: the Social Thought of Noam Chomsky" in *New Left Review* (Cohen & Rogers 1991). It's a useful short introduction to Chomsky's politics.

About the Author

Professor **Raphael Salkie** taught linguistics and translation at the University of Brighton for 40 years prior to his retirement in 2020. His interest in Noam Chomsky goes back to his first year as a university student when he found that learning about generative grammar (which wasn't on the syllabus) interested him more than his official studies. The author of 150 articles and two books, including *The Chomsky Update: Linguistics and Politics*, Salkie has written and lectured extensively about Chomsky over the years, and he has tried to challenge illegitimate authority whenever he could, as Chomsky has often advocated.

A Word from the Publisher

Thank you for reading *Simply Chomsky*!

If you enjoyed reading it, we would be grateful if you could help others discover and enjoy it too.

Please review it with your favorite book provider such as Amazon, BN, Kobo, Apple Books, or Goodreads, among others.

Again, thank you for your support and we look forward to offering you more great reads.

Printed in Great Britain
by Amazon

54554517R00101